MW00937364

GLIMMERS OF HOPE

*A Devotional Workbook for Navigating
the Struggles of Womanhood with Grace*

SIMONE DIGGS

Xulon
PRESS

INTRODUCTION

I dedicate this book to Mama—the perfect example of resilience and a woman who stays true to who she is and where she came from. Thank you for demonstrating what it means to stay anchored by faith when the ship starts to sink. Thank you for always giving me the extra push when I feel unworthy and incapable. Your strength, prayers, and encouragement have been the foundation of my every accomplishment.

And to any woman who is trying to walk hand in hand with the Lord on this rocky road called life: I know you stumble sometimes. Me too. Never forget that the rough patches do not determine who you are and Whose you are. God is beside you every step of the way.

INTRODUCTION

T his devotional workbook started with the simple vision of a quarter-of-a-century-aged gal from a sweet little town called Aiken in South Carolina. My short twenty-five years have been filled with tremendous adventure and a lot of unanticipated sorrow sprinkled in between. I do not claim to have passed all of the tests God has thrown my way with flying colors. In fact, I have admittedly tried to cheat my way through a few by detouring, following my own will and way, and taking the rocky road to some of life's destinations.

In spite of my twists, turns, and meanders, the Lord has been faithful. He has been the constant GPS system to help me navigate this life. Every roadblock I have met has served a purpose. That purpose has been to encourage other folks while encouraging myself.

"He comforts us in all our troubles so that we can comfort others. When they are troubled, we will be able to give them the same comfort God has given us" (2 Corinthians 1:4).

You see, Sister, we are all on this journey of life together. I don't know what your story is. My need to draw near to Christ began at a young age—a product of divorce, a father who struggled with alcoholism, and the abandonment and destruction that our family suffered as a result. That was just preparation for messier battles in adulthood, such as struggling with an anxiety disorder, surviving the suicide of my closest friend, unexpected heartbreak, and sudden rejection. Perhaps some of our struggles are relatable. Some of our other struggles may be too deep for another individual to fathom. Regardless of the roadblocks you have faced (or will face), I want to encourage you to keep pressing toward the ultimate destination—running into Jesus' arms and giving Him a big ole' hug in Heaven one day.

I don't claim to be a writer by trade. My thoughts are not profound; my words not unique. I spent a lot of years (and money) preparing for my current career as a counselor, but sometimes God wants us to fulfill a purpose beyond our nine-to-five. For whatever reason, He placed it on my heart to take my blogging hobby to the next level. He has led me to wipe away insecurities about my writing being inadequate and rest in the adequacy that comes with touching lives and helping people sail through their storms a little more gracefully. The words in this book choose to be heartfelt over being eloquent.

I want to know your story. I want to sit down with you over coffee, share testimonies, laugh, cry, and give hugs to one another. That would warm my heart in the sweetest of ways! For now, this is my way to reach out and touch you; to be a little glimmer of hope in a big, unpredictable world.

How to use this book

You have probably noticed that this is not your typical devotional book. I'm sure at least a few of you are thinking, *well this looks pretty wonky. There are barely enough pages to get me through the month, much less a year!* Before you shut this book and decide that I am out of my mind for the way it has been structured, please allow me to explain.

Devotional books have kept me encouraged through a lot of difficult times. If you are anything like me, you get excited at the thought of filtering some inspirational words into an otherwise chaotic day. I realized that my standard "one page per day" devotionals are either a hit or a miss. I often find myself turning the page, excited to read the words, only to realize that those words—no matter how wonderful—are not applicable to my current situation. As a result, I read the page, but I lack the fuel I need to power through my most burdensome struggle.

This devotional has a list of topics that inevitably impact women. I have designed it in such a way that you can use it as needed. I want you to be able to read the page that will speak truths that are relevant to your life and situation. Our struggles can change from day to day.

We are not alone in the feelings that we have, and we all need scriptural reminders that help us navigate those feelings.

For each topic listed, it is also my goal to help us discern between the lies that Satan feeds us and the truths that are in the Bible. Satan thrives off of consuming us with negative self-talk to distract us from the messages and blessings from the Lord. Sometimes we get inside of our own heads and give fuel to the fire that the enemy has started. The Bible tells us:

> *"The thief comes only to steal and kill and destroy. I came that they may have life and have it abundantly" (John 10:10).*

> *"Be sober-minded; be watchful. Your adversary the devil prowls around like a roaring lion, seeking someone to devour" (1 Peter 5:8).*

I don't know about you, but I want to be ready for battle when the enemy finds an open door into my heart. He knows us—our insecurities, our struggles, our vulnerabilities. He is just waiting to cripple us with lies and doubt. We do not have the strength to fight back without God on our side! Let's prepare for battle together.

> *"Put on the whole armor of God, that you may be able to stand against the schemes of the devil" (Ephesians 6:11).*

Before you dive in, please pray with me. We can't join hands, but let's close our eyes and bind our hearts in unity.

> *Father God, You are faithful in all of Your ways. Thank you for leading my sweet sisters to this devotional book. Lord, I pray that as each of us enter into personal battles with the enemy, that we keep our eyes on You. Please let the words in this book speak truth to each and every reader. Use each page to bring glory to Your goodness. Bless each reader*

and give them the strength to overcome their daily struggles. In Your perfect name we ask all of these things—Amen.

Remain hopeful. Stay anchored. Refuse to sink.
Sincerely,
Simone

ANGER

"Anger is an acid that can do more harm to the vessel in which it is stored than to anything on which it is poured." —Mark Twain

H ave you ever been the victim of a pot of water that boiled over? You are well aware that the stove is on high, fired up, and ready to do its job. However, you are so busy multitasking that you think it will be okay to leave the pot unattended. What can a few minutes away hurt? You'll tend to it a little later when you are finished marking a few other quick things off of your to-do list. Like any superwoman, you walk away to another task—brushing your teeth, throwing some clothes in the washer, tending to whining children, taking a phone call, ironing a shirt, or attempting to pick up a few toys and clothes off of the ground so you feel like there is at least a little tidiness left in your life. You've got it all figured out— right? Until you return to the kitchen and your stovetop has been transformed into a hot-water tsunami. You are left to clean up your mess (and suck up your superwoman pride). All of this could've been avoided if you would have just taken the time to be a little more cautious.

A similar danger arises when we fail to address our anger. Oftentimes we allow a person or circumstance to turn our burners on high. That coworker who has been slowly turning up the heat with offensive comments, that significant other who continues to annoy you with their bad habit, that kid who keeps on making the same mistake after you've reprimanded and redirected your brains out, that friend on social media who *always* has an insensitive post that makes you cringe. Our emotions start heating up—and rather than recognizing that those little unattended bubbles are the first sign of an imminent disaster, we decide to ignore the potential consequences. This only creates a chaotic situation that could've been avoided. The result of the chaos usually looks something like a loss of temper, an ugly heart, words of regret, hurt feelings, loss of respect from the party that made us angry, or a loss of dignity on our part when we realize that we failed to use self-control. Unlike the water on the stovetop that can be cleaned up with a little work, the consequences of our anger typically cannot be reversed.

Anger is a natural, acceptable, and inevitable emotion. The problem lies in the *actions and attitudes* that result from our anger. Perhaps your struggle is not acting irrationally out of anger. Perhaps your attitude is where the disaster lies. Someone or something makes you angry and you internalize it. You harbor bitter feelings toward that person or situation, and your heart hardens. Be sure not to underestimate the big mess that can be created by those harmless little bubbles that are left boiling and unattended.

Next time you feel the heat on your burner rising, go to God in prayer immediately. Only the Holy Spirit can provide us with the patience we need to demonstrate when others frustrate us. The Holy Spirit can also transform our hearts from the inside out, when our flesh desires to allow feelings of anger to determine our actions and attitudes.

Challenge:
1. **Identify your anger type.** Are you an *imploder* (person who internalizes feelings of anger and allows them to build up and destroy inner peace)? Or are you an *exploder* (person who allows anger to lead them to be reactionary and "blow up" on the people around them)?
2. **Replace imploding/exploding with introspection/ expanding.**
   - *Instead of imploding, shift your focus to introspection.* Consider what inner struggles might be brewing up and contributing to your anger. Are you upset about something that happened prior to the situation? Is it just an

off day for you? Are you emotionally drained with other things going on in your life? Furthermore, have you done an adequate job of communicating that a certain action is making you angry?

- *Replace exploding with expanding.* Expand your perspective of the person or thing that is causing you to become angry. If it is a person causing you anger, understand that there may be something going on in that person's life that is making them interact in an undesirable, unpleasant manner. Also consider that many individuals are ignorant of the fact that their behavior is causing someone else discontent. Extend them the grace and patience that you would want someone to extend you. If it is a situation that is making you angry, consider what unknown factors might be involved. We often take things personally and create scenarios and assumptions from our own lack of understanding. In addition to expanding our perspective, we need to expand our responses. Consider actions and attitudes that are more productive than anger; then adjust.

What Satan whispers to you in your anger:

"This person needs to know just how angry you are and why! Your tone and actions need to teach them a lesson. How will they really understand if you are not passionate in your delivery?"

"You have every right to be nasty toward this person, because they hurt you."

"You don't have to react, but you can be bitter toward them in the inside. Anger is okay if it's in your heart."

What God whispers to you in your anger:

"The Lord is merciful and gracious, slow to anger, and abounding in mercy. He will not always strive with us, nor will he keep His anger forever" (Psalm 103:8–9).

"Be angry, and do not sin. Do not let the sun go down on your wrath" (Ephesians 4:26).

"Let all bitterness, wrath, anger, clamor, and evil speaking be put away from you, with all malice" (Ephesians 4:31).

Food for thought: As Christians, our goal should be for our lives to look more like Christ each day. How can these verses direct us to deal with people who make us angry? If the people you interact with on a daily basis evaluated how you deal with anger, would they say you look more like Christ or Satan? When you evaluate your own heart, are you dealing with anger in a Godly manner?

Prayer for us: Heavenly Father, You are perfect. You give us guidelines to help us die to the flesh and look more like you. Please help us to not allow anger to consume us and sabotage our relationships. Help us to check our hearts frequently as we interact with others. In Your sweet name we ask these things—Amen.

ANXIETY

"Our anxiety does not come from thinking about the future, but from wanting to control it." —
Kahlil Gibran

In the book of 2 Corinthians, the apostle Paul speaks of having a "thorn in the flesh." *"So to keep me from becoming conceited because of the surpassing greatness of the revelations, a thorn was given me in the flesh, a messenger of Satan to harass me, to keep me from becoming conceited"* (2 Corinthians 12:7). Paul never goes into detail about what exactly this thorn was or looked like. However, we know that whatever it was, it served the dual purpose of plaguing him and humbling him.

Let us consider the elements of a thorn. Thorns are hard, with sharp, stiff ends. They are extensions of leaves, roots, and stems-typically serving the function of deterring animals from eating plant material. Now let us consider what it might feel like for a thorn to pierce our flesh. If you are anything like me, you stay as far as possible from anything that pricks you. One of my least favorite things is being poked with needles by a doctor, so the very thought of a thorn or any other object piercing my flesh makes my skin crawl. In most instances, you have a brief experience of discomfort, and then the sharp object is removed. Imagine what it would be like for that object to stick you *permanently*—no relief, no removal.

Anxiety is the thorn in the flesh of many individuals. For many of us, it persists day and night, regardless of our efforts to control it. We are plagued with a chronic case of the what-if's, and our minds always consider the worst-case scenario before the best. I'm not referencing the healthy amount of worry human beings should have. I am talking about the debilitating, life-consuming kind of worry—the kind where your brain can't seem to find the worry-off switch. This worry typically results from the fear of the unknown and the inability to control it. We begin to obsess over the details of our future—how long God is going to make us stay in this season of discontentment, what others will think of the product of our lives, if we are going to live up to our self-imposed expectations, when the people we love will start doing what we want them to do. Sometimes the obsessions are more focused on small, daily decisions—the danger of driving to a certain place, the fear of not having time to finish a project, the uncertainty of whether or not we are making everyone that we love happy. The lack of ability to foresee the details of the future manifests itself as physical distress and mental confusion.

If you have ever suffered from anxiety, you have probably asked God to remove it from your life on more than one occasion. Have you ever viewed your anxiety through the lens of a *blessing* rather than a curse? I know it is difficult to consider something that minimizes your fulfillment a blessing. However, anxiety could be that thorn in the flesh that hurts and humbles you simultaneously. Let's take a further look at the thorn in Paul's flesh. Paul demonstrated admirable endurance through a great deal of persecution and unfortunate circumstances, however, even he was honest with the Lord about wanting to flee his thorn.

> *"Three times I pleaded with the Lord about this, that it should leave me. But he said to me, 'My grace is sufficient for you, for my power is made perfect in weakness.' Therefore I will boast all the more gladly of my weaknesses, so that the power of Christ may rest upon me"* (2 Corinthians 12:8–9).

Just like us, Paul wanted out. He told the Lord he had enough of this thorn, but God's reaction was priceless. He reminded Paul that He had this situation, thorn and all, under control. This served as the encouragement Paul needed to embrace his weaknesses as a blessing and opportunity to cling closer to the cross.

God's power is the same now as it was when the apostle Paul pleaded for his thorn to be removed. He may not remove anxiety from our lives, but He can give us the strength we need to persevere. Peace to soothe our anxious minds awaits in the truths of the Gospel.

Challenge:
- Make a list of all of the things worrying you right now.
- As you review each worry, ask yourself if each worry is in your control.
- Contemplate whether or not you think any of the worries are too big for God to handle. *"Is anything too hard for the Lord?" (Genesis 18:14)*.
- Pray over your list of worries and ask God to equip you with the strength you need to fight them!

What Satan whispers to you when you are anxious:
"You are suffering alone in this battle of anxiety."
"These anxieties are bigger than God and you can't be so sure he will handle them."
"God is too busy to care about your worries."

What God whispers to you when you are anxious:

"Your mercy, O Lord, will hold me up. In the multitude of my anxieties within me, your comforts delight my soul" (Psalm 94:18–19).

"Look at the birds of the air: they neither sow nor reap nor gather into barns, and your heavenly Father feeds them. Are you not of more value than they? And which of you by being anxious can add a single hour to the span of life?.....Therefore do not be anxious about tomorrow, for tomorrow will be anxious for itself. Sufficient for the day is its own trouble" (Matthew 6:26–27; 34).

"Casting all of your anxieties on him, because he cares for you" (1 Peter 5:7).

"Do not be anxious about anything, but in everything by prayer and supplication with thanksgiving let your requests be made known to God. And the peace of God, which surpasses all understanding, will guard your hearts and your minds in Christ Jesus" (Philippians 4:6–7).

Food for thought: What anxieties has God placed in your life that have humbled you? How can we use our anxiety as a blessing to ourselves and others in our daily walk?

Prayer for us: Dear God—You are in control of all things. You give us thorns in the flesh that humble us and help us keep perspective of Your power. Lord, help us to live with our thorns, and use them as an asset. Give us that strength that You promise is made perfect in our weakness. We surrender all our anxieties and lay them at Your feet. We know that You care for us. Help us to speak Your truths to Satan when he challenges our flesh and our worry becomes out of control. In Your precious name—Amen.

BEAUTY

The beauty of a woman is not in a facial mode but the true beauty in a woman is reflected in her soul. It is the caring that she lovingly gives the passion that she shows. The beauty of a woman grows with the passing years." — Audrey Hepburn

I f you are a woman who has always felt beautiful every single day of her life, raise your hand! Please teach us your ways. Can we be transparent about this, Sisters? Our perceptions of beauty are fed to us before we can stand on two feet. We are given baby dolls with perfect little faces, perfect clothes, and perfect hair. We watch Disney princesses without one noticeable flaw prance in perfection across our television screens. We are bombarded with images of celebrities that make being beautiful seem as natural as breathing. Now, we even scroll through social media admiring the beauty of our friends and their friends. Advertisements and magazines meet our eyes as we stand in line to pay for groceries, teaching us how to be more attractive, eat healthier, age better, and live longer. (Then, we look down on and second-guess the choice of the chips, chocolate, and cookies in our buggy).

We sometimes hesitate to look in the mirror, because we fear noticing the one thing that we wish we could change. That one section of hair that will never follow the routine, the teeth that aren't straight or white enough, the few pounds we picked up that keep inviting more pounds to join the party, the wrinkles that keep giving themselves permission to sketch on our face, the skin that no regime can seem to make feel like a baby's bottom. Being critical of ourselves becomes so habitual that we begin to believe that other people see all of the "flaws" that we do.

We must remember that we were created in the image of God (Genesis 1:27). Take a moment to let that soak in. We *imperfect* human beings were made in the image of a *perfect* heavenly Father. That means that the Lord was intentional about making you and me. There was no mistake or nothing that could have been made better—down to the frizzy hair, those freckles, that birthmark, and those bigger bones. Sweet sister, we are only in our earthly bodies for a short time, because life is but a vapor that appears and vanishes away (James 4:14). Perfecting our image with a new diet, some makeup, or a skin routine is not going to get us any closer to heaven. Sure, it is okay to look our best and be confident, but that can't be our everything. We must refocus our time and energy into perfecting our souls. After all, a soul that has been perfected for God's purpose is the only route to salvation.

Challenge: Cover your mirror (or another place you see daily) with sticky notes that have positive messages and scriptures written on them. When your brain jumps to criticizing what you see in front of you, direct your attention to the messages you posted. We mimic what we meditate on. So the more that you review messages of truth, the more you will begin to believe the words.

What Satan whispers to you about beauty:
    "If you make a few changes to control how beautiful you are, your worth will be increased."
    "The flaws God created you with are hindering you from living abundantly."
    "What people see is their first impression of you. So that is most important."

What God whispers to you about beauty:

> *"Charm is deceptive, and beauty is fleeting; but a woman who fears the Lord is to be praised"*
> (Proverbs 31:30).

"I praise you for I am fearfully and wonderfully made; your works are wonderful, I know that full well" (1 Peter 3:3–4).

"Your beauty should not come from outward adornment, such as elaborate hairstyles and the wearing of gold jewelry or fine clothes. Rather it should be that of your inner self, the unfading beauty of a gentle and quiet spirit, which is of great worth in God's sight" (1 Peter 3:3–4).

Food for thought: What are your best attributes? If you asked your closest family and friends the things that they loved most about you, would their answers be relative to your inner or outer beauty?

Prayer for us: Our Father in Heaven, You knew just what you were doing when you made us. Thank You for creating us in Your perfect image. Thank You for being intentional about every feature that makes us who we are. Help us to not become consumed with our earthly appearance. Help us to use the energy we spend perfecting our outward selves to prepare our souls for heaven instead. In Jesus' name—Amen.

BROKEN-HEART

"I wish I were a little girl again, because skinned knees are easier to fix than broken heart." —
Julia Roberts

Many of us have childhood memories of cutting hearts out of construction paper—a little masterpiece created by folding your paper in half and using your top-notch scissor skills to cut one side. In a matter of seconds, voila! You have created a perfectly symmetrical heart. Somewhere between school and home, something happens to the heart if we don't put it in a safe place. We take the risk of placing it in a book bag under a hodgepodge of other items. We arrive home ready to show our creation, only to find that our once perfect heart is now folded, wrinkled, and ruined. We try every trick to smooth it out, fix it, and make it new, but the damage remains.

The physical hearts that God created us with are just as sensitive. Our hearts are full and innocent upon arriving into this world. Somewhere between birth and death, something happens to our hearts if we don't guard them. We take the risk of placing our hearts in the hands of other humans who we believe have our best interest in mind. Failed expectations and vulnerability leave our hearts shattered, twisted, and darkened. We try every remedy to distract us, soothe us, and heal us—but the damage remains.

Any time we choose to share our hearts with someone, we take a risk. Even the human beings that reciprocate our love have the capacity to hurt us, fail us, or leave us. In the midst of loving and being loved, we must be cautious of making any human being our

God. The Lord desires to be our first love. He wants our relationship with Him to be our top priority so that we can serve Him without distraction. Broken hearts are life interruptions that we can perceive as divine interventions. It is in our weakest moments that the Lord is near, welcoming us with open arms, teaching us to rely on Him, seek Him, cry on His shoulder, and be comforted by His promises. The damage of heartbreak never truly vanishes. However, if we make the decision to use our pain for purpose, God can remove pity and bitterness from our hearts and transform our brokenness into beauty.

Challenge:

- Make a list of the things that the person who broke your heart provides for you. Next, make a list of the things the Lord provides for you.
- Considering these lists, is there anything you can get from that person that the Lord does not provide?
- Circle the things on the lists that will provide long-term fulfillment.

What Satan whispers to your broken heart:

"This pain in your heart will cripple you forever."

"You need this relationship to complete you."

"You are too weak to handle this type of heartbreak."

What God whispers to your broken heart:

"He heals the brokenhearted and binds up their wounds" (Psalm 147:3).

"Not that I am speaking of being in need, for I have learned in whatever situation I am in to be content" (Philippians 4:11).

"My flesh and my heart may fail, but God is the strength of my heart and my portion forever" (Psalm 73:26).

Food for thought: What lesson is God teaching you through your heartbreak? Would you come to learn these things had your heart not been broken? How can you use this heartbreak as a beautiful testimony?

Prayer for us: Most gracious, heavenly Father, thank You for loving us abundantly. You are the perfect example of everlasting love. You are the One we can trust to guard our hearts and heal our brokenness. Help us to not fall victim to self-blame and bitterness when our hearts are broken. Be with the people who break our hearts and help them as well. Thank You for using our broken hearts to remind us that You are the only constant. You alone are our strength, hope, and shield. No human being compares to You. We praise You and ask all these things in Your name—Amen.

Glimmers of Hope

BURDENS

"God places the heaviest burden on those who can carry its weight." — Reggie White

Imagine you want to make it to an important destination and hiking through the woods is the only way to get there. You have been told about the awesome things that await you at the destination. You have been reassured that everything you need and more is there— every need and desire you can fathom is waiting on your arrival. However, there is a small part of you that is hesitant to believe this destination is all that it is cut out to be. So before you begin your journey on the path, you pack a "just in case" bag, full of items you might need along the way.

As you walk farther and farther along, the contents of the bag become heavy and uncomfortable, but you don't remove any items from the bag out of fear that they will not be there when you need them. You carry the weight and it begins to slow you down, making you weak and weary. By the time you make it to the destination, you are physically pained and drained. You put down your heavy load, only to look around and notice that all of the things you carried with you were indeed waiting at the destination.

After we accept Christ as our Savior, we cling to the promises of Heaven. We read about and sing of its perfection and majesty; no pain and no tears there. Still, doubt creeps into our hearts as we deal with our daily, earthly struggles. On our journey to eternity, we are not immune to suffering. Each day we bear our personal burdens— loss, financial turmoil, exhausting jobs, slow progress, difficult relationships, taking care of ourselves and others (and feeling that we could do more), failed expectations, and inadequacy. As we carry our own weight, the world adds more—inequality, injustice, terrorism, lack of resources, poor leadership, and the list goes on.

We inadvertently take on the weight of the world and internalize each problem. Our souls become troubled and we wonder if this whole being a believer thing is worth it. My friend, God did not promise that life as a Christian would be easy. However, He does promise us that He is with us as we force ourselves to persevere. Jesus Christ carried the biggest burden in history. As He walked, fragile and beaten, He carried all of our sins on his back. Even on the cross, He felt alone and heavy. *"My God, my God, why have you forsaken me?"* (Matthew 27:46). God was there with Him through the torture and was present in every drop of blood that stained the cross. In the end, the victory was present through the resurrection. Hallelujah!

Our victory and resurrection awaits on the other side. We must not lose sight of the destination we have been purposed for: Heaven. As we tarry on through this life, the Holy Spirit is walking with us, ready to pick us up when we fall. Let us pass our burdens over to Him.

Challenge: Write down all of the things that are weighing you down today. As you evaluate your list, pray over each burden and tell God that you are releasing it to Him.

What Satan whispers to you when you feel burdened:

"God is letting you suffer alone. He has given you all of these burdens and expects you to be strong enough to bear them yourself." "What if you break under pressure?"

"You can't be too sure that things will be better or that heaven is real."

What God whispers to you when you feel burdened:

"Come to me all who are weary and burdened, and I will give you rest. Take my yoke upon you and learn from me, for I am gentle and humble in heart, and

*you will find rest for your souls. For my yoke is easy
and my burden is light"* (Matthew 11:28–30).

*"Cast your burden on the Lord, and he will sustain
you; he will never permit the righteous to be moved"*
(Psalm 55:22).

*"For I consider that the sufferings of this present time
are not worth comparing with the glory that is to be
revealed to us"* (Romans 8:18).

Food for thought: What are some practical ways you can hand
your burdens over to the Lord on a daily basis? (Some ideas: account-
ability and prayer partners, setting aside a daily time to pray over
your burdens)

Prayer for us: Dear Lord, we worship You with all of our hearts
and minds right now. We need You. You have promised us that You
will bear our burdens in this life if we come to You for rest. Help us
to cling close by Your side as we walk through life's troubles, hand
in hand. Lord, help us to believe that Heaven is on the other side; a
perfect place that is void of suffering. Help us to not grow discouraged as we strive to reach the destination of ultimate fulfillment. In
Your name we ask these blessings—Amen.

COMFORT ZONES

"Life begins at the end of your comfort zone." —Neal
Donald Walsch

I t is a common desire for human beings to want to live abundantly.
We ponder the ways in which we can spend our days with purpose
and fulfillment—setting career goals, traveling the world, meeting
new people, and experiencing new things. We are 100% in favor of
changes that align with our plans. Sure, God, as long as the change
you are bringing our way matches one of the tiny boxes we can check
off our list of goals, bring it on!

Fear arises when God calls us to do something that we have no
intention of doing. When He interrupts our coffee-sippin' and plan-
makin' to take us to the wilderness, we wipe our hands clean. "God,
I didn't ask to do the dirty work!" We forget that progress comes
with a price—process. And all of a sudden, that great attitude we had
toward change turns into resistance.

God has called humankind to leave their comfort zones since the
beginning of time. One of the greatest examples of this is demonstrated through Abraham's story in the Old Testament. Abraham was
seventy-five years old. At that age, most people are transitioning into
a well-deserved life of comfort, routine, and newfound relaxation.
Little did Abraham know, God had a different plan in mind.

God commanded Abraham, *"Leave your country and your
people. Leave your father's family. Go to the land I will show you. I
will make you into a great nation. I will bless you. I will make your
name great. You will be a blessing to others. I will bless those who*

bless you. I will put a curse on anyone who curses you. All nations on earth will be blessed because of you" (Genesis 12:1–3).

Put yourself in Abraham's shoes. "Wait a minute, God—you want me to just leave everybody and everything I know? At seventy-five years old? You are calling me to go to an unknown place with an unknown purpose for a few promises I can't even see?" That would be my reaction.

Immediately after, verse 4 tells us, *"Abraham departed as the Lord had spoken to Him."* There was no questioning God's plan. There was no resistance or refusal. There was no sitting and pouting. Abraham went without hesitation. He stepped out of his seventy-five year old established comfort zone and fulfilled his God-given purpose. It may have been over the course of hundreds of years, but God fulfilled all of His promises to Abraham.

Are we faithful enough to put our excuses on the backburner, throw our comfort out of the window, and do what God is calling us to do? Some of us might be kicking our feet up and reclining, waiting for the abundance of our life to just happen on its own. Others of us know that God is calling us to make a move, but we are digging our feet into the ground- reluctant to step forward into the abundant life promised to us. God had a plan for Abraham and He has a plan for us. Refusing to allow Him to use us might negatively impact our lives and the lives of other people with whom God wants us to share our gifts and talents.

Challenge:
- Write down the thing that God is calling you to do that you are resisting.
- Next, make a list of at least three pros and three cons to following through.
- How might staying in your comfort zone negatively impact your future?

What Satan whispers about comfort zones:
"Leaving your comfort zone may not be worth it. Besides, you will be alone on a journey that may not even be successful."
"Being comfortable where you're at is the best and safest decision."
"Who's to say that God won't leave you hanging?"

What God whispers about comfort zones:

> *"Have I not commanded you? Be strong and coura-*
> *geous. Do not be frightened, and do not be dismayed,*
> *for the Lord your God is with you wherever you go"*
> (Joshua 1:9).

> *"Then Jesus told his disciples, 'If anyone would come*
> *after me, let him deny himself and take up his cross*
> *and follow me"* (Matthew 16:24).

> *"And I will lead the blind in a way that they do not*
> *know, in paths they have not known I will guide them.*
> *I will turn the darkness before them into light, the*
> *rough places into level ground. These are the things*
> *I do, and I do not forsake them"* (Isaiah 42:16).

Food for thought: What would the impact have been if Jesus chose his comfort zone over the cross?

Prayer for us: Gracious and loving Father, we welcome You into our lives. You have a plan for each one of us. You have an abundant life of possibilities waiting for us, if we accept the challenge. We know that You have given us free will. We confess that we need help stepping out of our comfort zones to do what You are calling us to. Help us to consider how ignoring Your call might impact us and the people who need us. Help us to have the courage to step out and serve our purpose. We ask these things in Your son's name—Amen.

DEPRESSION

"You largely constructed your depression. It wasn't given to you. Therefore, you can deconstruct it." — Albert Ellis

I f you have ever been depressed or are currently depressed, you recognize that it does not happen overnight. As the world weighs on you gradually, the days darken. It begins as a cloudy haze and before you know it, you are in a pitch-black pit with what seems like no escape. The pit itself is not the scariest part—being alone in the pit is. You cry out for help, only to hear the echo of your own voice in response.

My friend, you are not alone. Do not make the mistake of believing that your depression makes you inhuman. Since the beginning of time, humankind has battled these feelings of darkness. It is no coincidence that God chose to provide us with examples of biblical characters who endured depression and despair.

One of the most thorough examples is found in the book of Job. Job was an upright man who was blameless in the sight of the Lord. However, that did not stop Satan from afflicting him and God from allowing him to endure the affliction. If you have ever gotten bad news, you know that your heart feels like it drops into your stomach. Well, if there was a world record for most back-to-back bad news, our friend Job would be the winner—hands down! He suffered the loss of all his livestock, the destruction of his home, his servants wiped clean, and the tragic death of all ten of his children, simultaneously. Everything he had worked for and tended to was lost in the blink of an eye, leaving him with not much more than his own body. Surely this was rock bottom for Job, right? Not quite. As if things could get any worse, Job was smitten with boils on his body from head to toe. Somehow, Job found the strength to remain optimistic in the Lord when he first began suffering losses, but it was not long before these afflictions drove him into a state of hopelessness—emotionally drained, physically tired, and mentally unwell. Chapter 7 opens with Job's complaints, *"Like a slave longing for the evening shadows, or a hired laborer waiting to be paid, so I have been allotted months of futility and nights of misery have been assigned to me. When I lie down I think, 'How long before I get up?' The night drags on, and I toss and turn until dawn. My body is clothed with worms and scabs, my skin is broken and festering. My days are swifter than a weaver's shuttle, and they come to an end without hope. Remember, O God, that my life is but a breath; my eyes will never see happiness again"* (Job 7:2–7).

Have you ever felt that way? The days seem to drag and you are just going through the motions? You long for happiness but the possibilities of attaining it seem bleak?

A few verses later, Job begins to question the Lord. *"What is humankind that you make so much of them, that you give them so much attention, that you examine them every morning and test them every moment? Will you never look away from me, or let me alone even for an instant? If I have sinned, what have I done to you, you who sees everything we do? Why have you made me your target? Have I become a burden to you? Why do you not pardon my offenses and forgive my sins?"* (Job 7:17–21).

Five verses of questioning God. We tend to express similar frustration in our circumstances. "God, why me? Why are You choosing to make me go through this pain? What have I done to deserve this? When will I experience relief from this affliction?"

I wish that I could say God responded to Job immediately. Nope. He had to suffer until his heart was ready for the response. That response does not happen until way down in chapter 40.

God responds:

> *"Would you discredit my justice? Would you condemn me to justify yourself? Do you have an arm*

like God's and can your voice thunder like his? Then adorn yourself with glory and splendor, and clothe yourself in honor and majesty. Unleash the fury of your wrath, look at all who are proud and bring them low, look at all who are proud and humble them, crush the wicked where they stand. Bury them all in the dust together; shroud their faces in the grave. Then I myself will admit to you that your own right hand can save you" (Job 40:8–14).

God reminded Job of His power and it humbled him. When it was all said and done, Job was blessed with 140 more years of life, new possessions, and the opportunity to witness four generations of his family. Notice that it was not until he passed his test and stopped questioning God's plan that he was able to reap the blessings that the Lord had in store for him.

Sometimes life takes us to a dark place like the one Job experienced. Personal loss, job loss, broken relationships and friendships, abuse, addiction, failed expectations, or a combination of many of these things can lead us down the path of hopelessness. Like Job, we can only take so much before we get frustrated with waiting for the Lord to intervene; to reach his mighty hand down and pull us out of the pit. In the midst of our storms, we must recognize that better days await us. More importantly, we must never question the Lord. He makes the earth spin on its axis, places the sun, moon, and stars in the sky, takes care of every creature in the universe and still makes time to care about you and me. If any one of us believes we are more powerful or all-knowing than a God like that, then let's go try and figure our lives out and see how that turns out.

We must make the choice to find the beauty in every ugly situation. There is always something to praise our Lord for, and if you are reading this, you already have one thing to show gratitude for— life. Each day is a new opportunity to take a step toward recovery and optimism. It will not be an easy or short journey, and you might have to wait until Chapter 40 of your story until it all begins to make sense. God's blessing is at the end, just waiting for you to pass the test and obtain it.

Challenge: If you are battling depression, be transparent in admitting to someone that you are struggling. Then, seek professional help. If you have a church home, confide in a religious leader who can pray with and for you.

What Satan whispers when you are depressed:
"The God you are crying out to is not listening."
"The suffering in your life feels like the end of the world and it is not going to get better."
"All hope is gone."
"You have no reason to rejoice."

What God whispers when you are depressed:

> *"I waited patiently for the Lord; he inclined to me and heard my cry. He drew me up from the pit of destruction, out of the miry bog, and set my feet upon a rock, making my steps secure. He put a new song in my mouth, a song of praise to our God. Many will see and fear, and put their trust in the Lord"* (Psalm 40:1–3).

> *"I have said these things to you, that in me you may have peace. In the world you will have tribulation. But take heart; I have overcome the world!"* (John 16:33).

> *"But he who is joined with all the living has hope, for a living dog is better than a dead lion"* (Ecclesiastes 9:4).

> *"But rejoice insofar as your share Christ's sufferings, that you may also rejoice and be glad when his glory is revealed"* (1 Peter 4:13).

Food for thought: Philippians 4:8 says, "Finally brothers, whatever is true, whatever is honorable, whatever is just, whatever is pure, whatever is lovely, whatever is commendable, if there is any excellence, if there is anything worthy of praise, think about these things."

How can meditating on these things help to transform our thoughts?

Prayer for us: Dear God in Heaven, we love You. You are the God of the Universe who keeps all things in order accordingly. We recognize Your power. We know that there is no state of mind You cannot transform for the better. We thank You for another day of life and another chance to grasp hope. Help us to have the patience we need to persevere through the tribulations in this world. Help us to combat our depression with gratitude and praise. We ask all of these blessings in Your name—Amen.

DISCONTENTMENT

"Content makes poor men rich. Discontent makes rich men poor." —Benjamin Franklin

We live in a generation that is plagued with a spiritual disease of discontentment. Humans have always had a flesh that is constantly desiring more. However, today's society has exasperated this natural desire. We are exposed to the lives of other people through social media and television—what they are accomplishing, what they have, what their exciting plans for the future are. Then the flesh begins to create voids in our hearts that did not even exist before.

We treat our flesh like a large, empty bucket, seeking to fill it with meaningless affirmations and acceptance from others. We distract ourselves by taking on more duties, buying more things, and striving for more goals. While we are expecting our buckets to overflow with fulfillment from this world, something contrary results. Our buckets turn into funnels. Instead of filling us up, the contents quickly make their way through one end and out of the other, leaving us completely empty, disappointed, and discontent.

No matter how many insignificant things we pour into the flesh, it will never be satisfied. We should focus our minds and energy on spiritual things. Eternal life cannot be accomplished by chasing temporary things. Keep in mind that discontentment is not contingent upon what we are lacking, but the inability to recognize and appreciate what we already have. What a wonderful truth to know that becoming content is a *choice* that can be controlled by our perspective!

Our Lord is watching us run from well to well; exhausted, with buckets still empty. He is just waiting for us to come to Him so that he can quench every void that is thirsting for fulfillment. It is only in His arms that we will grow content and find the peace that we are tirelessly seeking.

Challenge:
- Starting today, keep a daily gratitude record of the things you are thankful for. Anytime that you feel discontent, revisit the blessings you have been writing down.
- Go to God in prayer, not asking Him for anything more, but rather thanking Him for all that He has already provided.

What Satan whispers about discontentment:
"You have to find your own joy in this world."
"Do whatever brings you satisfaction."
"You need to be hungry for your dreams and focus all of your energy into those things."

What God whispers about discontentment:

"You make known to me the path of life; in your presence there is fullness of joy; at your right hand are pleasures forevermore" (Psalm 16:11).

"And the Lord will guide you continually and satisfy your desire in scorched places and make your bones strong; and you shall be like a watered garden, like a spring of water, whose waters do not fail" (Isaiah 58:11).

"But whoever drinks of the water that I will give him will never be thirsty again. The water that I will give him will become in him a spring of water welling up to eternal life" (John 4:14). "Blessed are those who hunger and thirst for righteousness, for they shall be satisfied" (Matthew 5:6).

Food for thought: In what have you been investing most of your energy in order to be fulfilled lately? What would happen if you took that time and spent it with the Lord instead?

Prayer for us: Dear Lord, thank You for the opportunity for us to sit in Your presence. We are so grateful for all of the blessings You have given us and we want to give You praise! We confess that we have been discontent and repent of our ungrateful hearts. Help us to know that we are enough, have enough, and are doing enough if we have You. You are sufficient. You are all that we need. Help us to make the choice to be happy with what we have and to resist our fleshly desires for more. We pray these things in Your name—Amen.

Glimmers of Hope

ENEMIES

"Love is the only force capable of transforming an enemy into a friend." —Martin Luther King, Jr.

There are few things that can steal our joy the way that people bondage can. People bondage is allowing other people's thoughts and opinions toward us dictate our mindsets and behaviors. We become sensitive and reactive to the negativity that others place on us.

Having enemies in this life is inevitable, regardless of how blamelessly we seek to live. Due to the fact that we live in a sinful society, others will find reasons to hate us, even if it be because of our faith in Jesus Christ. The existence of enemies can actually be one of the best ways to develop Christ-like traits. Enemies are watching the way we deal with circumstances. They want to see how we react to pain, disappointment, and failure. They are often waiting to watch us fall from the higher ground that we have chosen.

Unfortunately, Satan can create enemies out of people that we have to interact with regularly. Maybe it is a coworker who causes disputes. It may even be a person in our family. Regardless of the circumstance, these individuals thrive on our reactions and feedback. Like a seed that is planted and watered, the more we entertain our enemies with hatred, the more the attacks grow.

We are called to be lights in this dark, hateful world. Jesus Christ gave us the perfect example of how to interact with enemies. He was persecuted by many, hated without reason, and crucified in spite of His perfection. No matter how many times Satan tempted Him with attacks from others, He chose to walk in love. He did not allow hatred and negative energy to harden His heart. He committed himself to truth, even if it costed Him popularity with the majority.

What is even more admirable is that Jesus had the right *heart* toward His enemies. Oftentimes, we are able to resist the urge to act rudely in response to our enemies. However, our heart toward them remains wicked. We force smiles and bite our tongues, but on the inside, we harbor secret hatred and ill will.

Did you know that responding to our enemies in love could plant a seed that leads them to Christ? It is difficult to fathom this truth, but we should be concerned with saving the souls of *all* people—not just those who we get along with. Our reaction to attacks should leave our enemies wondering what makes us different, because our life is a reflection of the Gospel. Remember that one negative response to an enemy could mean a soul that is lost.

Challenge: Examine your heart to consider the feelings and thoughts you are having toward your enemies. Repent of any negative thoughts that have come to your mind or have come out in your actions. Recognizing your own sin will free you and benefit your future interactions with your enemies.

What Satan whispers about enemies:
"Sit back and watch them get what they deserve."
"If you are not careful, your enemies could bring you down."
"Put them in their place! They offended you!"

What God whispers about enemies:

"Do not gloat when your enemy falls; when they stumble, do not let your heart rejoice" (Proverbs 24:17).

"Though I walk in the midst of trouble, you preserve my life. You stretch out your hand against the anger of my foes; with your right hand you save me" (Psalm 138:7).

"Let your light shine before men so that they may see your good works and glorify your Father in Heaven" (Matthew 5:16).

Food for thought: What messages are you sending to your enemies when they offend or attack you? What would you like to do more or less of in response to their attacks? Create a plan for how you will respond the next time you are attacked.

Prayer for us: Oh Lord, we humble ourselves before You. We thank You for all of those that love us and also for those that hate us. God, we know that we have a responsibility to be the light in this dark world. Help us to walk in love when it is hard to. Help us to pray for our enemies instead of reacting to them. Let us always be about the business of saving all of the souls that we can. We need Your direction in navigating these things and we ask these things in Your name—Amen.

ENVY

"The spirit of envy can destroy; it can never build." —
Margaret Thatcher

There is a sinister spirit that lurks within us and buries itself behind other feelings. Unlike many other emotions, it does not always manifest into action. Instead, it eats away silently at our souls, snatches our peace, and squeezes our hearts. This is the spirit of envy.

Envy is when we feel resentment aroused by another person's desirable possessions or qualities, accompanied by an intense desire to have them for ourselves. Oftentimes, we are envious of situations that we don't really understand. We are dictated by a surface-level view of a person or thing that appears so appealing, but we have no concept of what lies beneath.

"I want her marriage."

"I want her perfect mommy skills."

"I want her awesome, successful career."

"I want her fit and healthy lifestyle."

"I want her creativity."

Satan deceives us into thinking we see a picture of perfection that we begin to desire for ourselves. My friend, this is a *lie*. No person, situation, or thing on this earth will ever be perfect. We *all* struggle with those quiet demons that the world does not see. We are *all* broken and imperfect. If any one of us was perfect, then this world would not need a Savior. That is precisely why our focus should be on serving our perfect, heavenly Father.

One of the significant roots of envy is entitlement—believing that we have a right to something. We often try our best to be good people and think that life owes us perfect circumstances in return. If we are giving it our all, shouldn't things look better in our relationships, careers, lifestyles, and so forth? The truth is that we do not deserve anything. We are blessed with what we do have by God's grace and mercy alone. The more we fall victim to feelings of entitlement, the more we open a door for Satan to plant a seed of envy in our hearts.

There are a few practical steps that can help us to overcome the spirit of envy:

1. **Accept that we struggle with envious feelings**—we need to accept these feelings as a true problem that is stealing our joy.
2. **Repent for our sins**—although envy is a natural, fleshly response, we must repent so that the Lord can begin to cleanse us from these feelings and help us to move forward.
3. **Accept ourselves as we are**—the Bible teaches us that we all have unique, God-given gifts and should use them to benefit one another (see 1 Peter 4:10 and Romans 12:6).
4. **Keep perspective of what matters**—ultimately, if we are in Christ, we have the greatest gift that exists. Salvation is a better gift than any other, and it is given to us equally as we accept Christ!
5. **Uplift the people who elicit the feelings of envy**—the bible teaches us to "rejoice with those who rejoice" (Romans 12:15). If somebody has something good, we can be genuinely happy for them and realize that we have good things in our lives, too.
6. **Remember that the surface is not the whole story**—Reminder: The very people we are envious of are fighting their own demons that we cannot see.

Challenge: Take some time to evaluate the six steps that are given above. Apply them to each situation or person you are envious of, so that you can free your heart and mind to move forward.

What Satan whispers to you about envy:
"It is natural to be envious and okay, because nobody has to know."

"Wanting what they have will help you not to grow complacent."
"The things they have are important."

What God whispers to you about envy:

> *"A heart at peace gives life to the body, but envy rots the bones"* (Proverbs 14:30).

> *"For what does it profit a man if he gains the whole world, but loses his soul?"* (Luke 9:25).

> *"Since, then, you have been raised with Christ, set your hearts on things above, where Christ is, seated at the right hand of God. Set your mind on things above, not on earthly things"* (Colossians 3:1–2).

Food for thought: What blessings (physical or spiritual) might result when you free yourself of envy?

Prayer for us: Our loving Father in Heaven, thank You for everything You provide us. Thank You for blessing us abundantly, even when we fail to show gratitude. Help us to overcome the ugly spirit of envy. Help us to not fall victim to social comparison and entitlement. We want to desire You and You alone—not things, not other people's lifestyles. We repent of the envy in our hearts and we release it to You. Help these envious feelings to be replaced with more productive ones. In Your name we declare these things—Amen.

FAITH

"Faith is taking the first step, even when you can't see the whole staircase." —Martin Luther King, Jr.

I f there was a poll given to identify the favorite word used among Christians, "faith" would likely be the winner. We speak of it daily in our Christian colloquialisms, post about it on social media, and sing about it in church, but are our lives a *true* reflection of what it means to have faith?

To have faith is to have *complete* trust and confidence in someone or something. Notice the emphasis on the word *complete*. As Christians, this implies that we should completely trust in God and the promises He gives us in His word. Hebrews 11:6 tells us that, *"without faith it is impossible to please God."* God is not pleased with us when our faith is half-hearted. He is not interested in us professing our faith if it is merely 50%, 80%, 99.9%. He calls us to have 100% faith in our daily walk with Him.

There is a demon who is at war with our faith—his name is doubt. Doubt is Satan's weapon to constantly battle the faith that the Holy Spirit has worked so hard to instill in us. Did you know that doubting is actually a sin? *"But whoever has doubts is condemned if he eats, because the eating is not from faith. For whatever did not proceed from faith is sin" (Romans 14:23).* Faith can take us to places far greater than we can fathom. Doubt can be equally as powerful and send us back to square one.

Let us consider a few biblical contrasts between faith and doubt. Our powerful Jesus walked on the sea as His disciples watched in amazement from the boat. Peter, one of the disciples, wanted Jesus to confirm His identity by allowing him to walk on the water, too. He had enough faith to get off of the boat as the Lord commanded him and begin walking on the water toward Jesus.

> *"But when he saw the wind was boisterous, he was afraid; and beginning to sink he cried out saying, 'Lord save me!' And immediately Jesus stretched out His hand and caught him, and said to him, 'O you of little faith, why did you doubt?" (Matthew 14:30–31).*

We notice that in faith, Peter was able to do something he never imagined, but as soon as he began to doubt, he failed. Isn't that how we are today? We start on the path to attaining beautiful blessings and then allow doubt to drown us. I wonder how many miracles Jesus could perform in our lives if our faith allowed Him to do so?

An example of the faith we need to strive for is seen in another New Testament story. Jesus was walking with His disciples. *"And suddenly, a woman who had a flow of blood for twelve years came from behind and touched the hem of his garment. For she said to herself, 'If only I may touch his garment, I shall be made well.' But Jesus turned around, and when He saw her He said, 'Be of good cheer, daughter, your faith has made you well.' And the woman was made well from that hour" (Matthew 9:20–22).*

I don't know about you, but I want to have a faith that big. A faith so big, that I believe just a simple cry out to the Savior can change my situation. A faith so big that God can sense my presence among the multitude of people crying out to Him.

Hebrews 13:8 tells us that, *"Jesus Christ is the same yesterday, today, and forever."* Jesus may not be physically present, but we have been blessed with the Holy Spirit dwelling within us, giving us full access to Him through faith and prayer. What a joy to know that today we have access to the same God who caused men to walk on water, healed the sick with just one touch, raised the dead, and performed countless other miracles.

Challenge:
- Consider the most prominent area of doubt in your mind right now. On a scale of 1–10 (1 being the lowest and 10 being the highest), where does your level of faith fall right now?
- Make a plan to move yourself up on the scale. (Ideas: praying multiple times of day over that specific doubt, writing faith scriptures on a card to carry with you and meditate throughout the day).

What Satan whispers about faith:
"Stop praying for something that is not tangible."
"Be realistic. Doubts help you to protect yourself and avoid being disappointed."
"How can you believe in what you cannot see?"

What God whispers about faith:

> *"What is impossible with men is possible with God" (Luke 18:27).*

> *"But let him ask in faith with no doubting, for he who doubts is like a wave of the sea, driven and tossed by the wind" (James 1:6).*

> *"Now faith is the assurance of things hoped for, the conviction of things not seen" (Hebrews 11:1).*

Prayer for us: Dear God, You are the worker of all miracles. You give us examples of Your power in Your word to keep us encouraged for generations. Thank You for giving us faith as a way to access You 24/7. Lord, we know that Satan wants to make us doubt Your power. He wants us to doubt that You are real and You are able. We need Your help increasing our faith to 100% so that we do not fall victim to doubt. We know that blessings await us if we truly believe in Your promises. In Your name we pray—Amen.

Glimmers of Hope

FORGIVENESS

"It's one of the greatest gifts you can give yourself, to forgive. Forgive everybody." —Maya Angelou

Hurt and betrayal are inevitable facets of this life. At some point, we have all been on the giving or receiving end of forgiveness. When we are seeking forgiveness from someone, we are desperately hoping that they take our words and actions genuinely. We pray for them to take our apologies seriously and see the heart change we have had. We are anxious about the fact forgiveness is in the control of another person, increasing the chance for a relationship to be severed. When we are attempting to forgive someone, things can be equally as challenging. We are weary of letting our guards down to trust the person who hurt us. We pray that their hearts have truly changed and that it is not just a façade to help them get what they desire. We are anxious about the fact that we could be setting ourselves up for the same disappointment to reoccur.

When the time comes for us to give forgiveness, we mistakenly forget what it's like to be on the other end of the bargain. The goal of the Christian should be to have a life that reflects more of Christ every day. We must not allow the inability to forgive to deter us from that goal. We often justify our hesitation to forgive with excuses about how we trusted the person, how we feel victimized, and why we do not deserve the treatment they gave us. While it may be true that we did not bring the negative actions upon ourselves, we still have to forgive. Why? Because God commands that we do so.

Jesus Christ gave us the perfect example of granting forgiveness in the midst of difficult circumstances. Jesus walked blamelessly on this earth—sinless, compassionate, and never once wronging others. When Jesus was seized, even Pilate professed that he could find nothing Jesus did that was deserving of death. Our Lord was betrayed regardless. His own people mocked Him and insisted that He be crucified, and as Jesus hung in turmoil, undeservingly bound to an old rugged cross, He found it in His heart to forgive. *"Father forgive them for they know not what they do" (Luke 23: 34).*

I do not know who you are having trouble forgiving today, my friend. Maybe it is hitting close to home—your best friend, your parents, your siblings, your children, or your spouse. The wrongs committed against us are not nearly as terrible as the crucifixion of Jesus Christ. How powerful would it be if we had a Christ-like attitude toward forgiveness in our situations?

Challenge: Author Gary Chapman made the statement that, "Forgiveness does not destroy our memory." If you have decided to forgive but find the wrongdoing creeping up in your memory, take the following steps:

1. Go to God in prayer and acknowledge that you are remembering these negative thoughts.
2. Ask God to help you do something that will promote moving forward.

What Satan whispers to us about forgiveness:
   "What is the point of forgiving them?"
   "They keep messing up over and over again, so why trust them again?"
   "They have hardened your heart and you have every right to hesitate to forgive them."

What God whispers to us about forgiveness:

> *"For if you forgive other people when they sin against you, your heavenly father will forgive you also" (Matthew 6:14).*

"Then Peter came to and said to Him, 'Lord, how often shall my brother sin against me and I forgive him? Up to seven times?' Jesus said to him, 'I do not say to you, up to seven times, but up to seventy times seven" (Matthew 18:21–22).

"Be kind to one another, tender-hearted, forgiving each other, just as God in Christ has also forgiven you" (Ephesians 4:32).

Food for thought: Studies show that there are health benefits to forgiveness, such as decreased stress and anxiety, lower blood pressure, fewer symptoms of depression, and improved heart health. What physical symptoms might be manifesting as a result of your inability to forgive?

Prayer for us: Our Father in Heaven, You are perfect. You forgive us when we fall short time and time again. You are patient with us and always ready to welcome us back to Your presence with open arms. Lord, help us to treat other people with the same attitude. When they wrong us, help us to show them the grace that You show to us, daily. We repent of the bitterness we have in our hearts and release it in Your name—Amen.

Glimmers of Hope

GRIEF

*"Grief is in two parts. The first is loss. The second is
the remaking of life."* —Anne Rophie

There is no moment we feel more isolated in this world than
when we lose a person we love. I will not claim to know what
your situation is or the capacity of your loss. Maybe you lost a dear
friend or loved one. Maybe your loss came in the form of a job or a
pet, or perhaps you are grieving the loss of a relationship that was
vital to your life. Regardless of the specific circumstances, there are
truths that we must remember in the midst of our pain. I know it
hurts. I know it stings your heart in a way that nothing else does. I
know you are longing to be able to reverse the situation, to avoid the
suffering. I know that a part of you has been lost—a piece of your
heart's puzzle can never be replaced. Hang in there, sweet friend. Let
us consider these things:

1. God understands your pain when nobody else does.
You may be feeling that God is far from you right now. Maybe
you are blaming Him for taking that special someone or something
away. It is possible you are even bargaining with him to bring it/them
back. In actuality, God is closer to you now than ever before. Psalm
34:18 tells us that, *"The Lord is near to the brokenhearted and saves
the crushed in spirit."* Other people may be attempting to comfort
you with their stories of loss and survival, but no two losses are the
same. We were created in the image of the Lord, meaning that our
emotions are experienced by Him as well. He knows all and sees

all. He understands the magnitude of your loss and he is waiting to embrace you. I know it is difficult to conceptualize, but we must be careful to not turn away from Him in these moments of despair. Loss is a part of this earthly life, but God remains as our constant.

2. Embrace the journey, don't drown in it.

Grieving is a natural process. After you have accepted your loss, you can begin picking up the pieces and become acclimated to your new normal. Be careful to not run away from this season of grieving. It is okay to cry and be deeply saddened. John 11:35 tells us that, *"Jesus wept."* Our Lord, our perfect Savior cried when He lost His dear friend. Do not feel obligated to hide your tears and force a smile. Embrace the rough journey, but beware of drowning in the midst of it all. When we are experiencing grief, we are also extremely vulnerable. Satan would love to keep you in this low place forever, so that he can win you over in your despair. Fight back. Remember that better days are ahead and you can make the choice to find hope in the future. There is a bigger picture—an eternal home, free of suffering, in our future.

> *"So we do not lose heart. Though our outer self is wasting away, our inner self is being renewed day by day. For this light momentary affliction is preparing us for an eternal weight of glory, beyond all comparison, as we look not to the things that are seen but the things that are unseen. For the things that are seen are transient, but the things that are unseen are eternal" (2 Corinthians 4: 16–18).*

3. Spread love as a tool in recovery.

Although our hearts can be sensitive and easily broken, God made our hearts resilient as well. No matter how much hurt we experience, He has given us the capability to continue to love. Grieving is one of the most important times to love. It is easy to feel as though we are being punished and easy for our hearts to harden. To combat this, we must realize that this life is not all about us and our happiness. The people and things we have the opportunity to love are given to us through God's grace, not because we earned or deserve it. Experiencing loss should encourage us to appreciate the people and things that remain. As Christians, God has given us a purpose to love others as a representative of Him. That purpose does not change, even when our circumstances do. When spreading love to other people becomes a part of our lifestyle, we dwell less on our own problems.

Challenge: Write down a few thoughts about what you would like to learn, during this season of grieving. Revisit the list often to acknowledge the things that have gotten better and the things you still need to work on with time.

What Satan whispers about grief:
"God is far from you, because he is making you grieve."
"There is no hope in this loss."
"You are in this alone."

What God whispers about grief:

> *"For I am sure that neither death nor life, nor angels nor rulers, nor things present nor things to come, nor powers, nor height nor depth, nor anything else in all creation, will be able to separate us from the love of God in Christ Jesus our Lord" (Romans 8:38–39).*

> *"But we do not want you to be uninformed, brothers, about those who are asleep, that you may not grieve as others do who have no hope" (1 Thessalonians 4:13).*

> *"The LORD is my shepherd; I shall not want. He makes me lie down in green pastures. He leads me beside still waters. He restores my soul.*

> *He leads me in paths of righteousness for his name's sake. Even though I walk through the valley of the shadow of death, I will fear no evil,*

for you are with me; your rod and your staff, they comfort me. You prepare a table before me in the presence of my enemies; you anoint my head with oil; my cup overflows. Surely goodness and mercy shall follow me all the days of my life and I shall dwell in the house of the LORD forever" (Psalm 23).

Food for thought: God has blessed us abundantly, regardless of the losses we experience. What things remain in your life that you can be thankful for?

Prayer for us: Our Father in Heaven, You are the source of strength. Thank You for being a constant comfort to us. Lord, our hearts are hurting. Help us to find the strength to make it through each day knowing that You are near to us. Help us to spread love and use us for Your purpose in the midst of our pain. Let us never forget the power of Your words and Your promises. Help us to live in such a way that we might make Heaven our home someday. In Your name we ask these things—Amen.

GUILT

"Guilt is to the Spirit what pain is to the body." —
David Bednar

I t can be crippling—that sick feeling that comes over you when you think of your intentional wrongdoing. You lost the battle to your flesh, and now you cannot seem to get over it. That lie you told, that person you wronged, that guilty pleasure you indulged in. No matter how far you push it to the back of your mind, it makes its way to the forefront with a vengeance.

Guilt opens the perfect little door for Satan to enter our hearts and make us feel unworthy and ashamed. He thrives in our moments of self-loathing, because it is the perfect opportunity to feed us lies. He leads us to believe that if people only knew the truth about our struggles, they wouldn't love us. Suddenly, it feels as if we are exposed, like the entire world is looking at our sin through a magnifying glass.

We attempt to ignore guilt by running away and consuming ourselves with other things, only to find that it is still in the corner waiting to greet us in the dark hours. The feeling of guilt can manifest into serious mental health concerns when we are not careful. Guilt makes us more susceptible to stress, anxiety, and depression. In the Bible, Judas felt so guilty for betraying Jesus that his remorse led to him hang himself. Satan can fool us into thinking that living in guilt is not worth living at all, leaving us hopeless.

The good news is that we have an escape. There is One who came to pay the price so that grace could trump our guilt. Jesus said, *"The thief comes only to steal and kill and destroy. I came that they may have life and have it abundantly" (John 10:10).* Our Savior is waiting for us to free ourselves of past mistakes, self-disgust, and condemnation. He deeply desires for us to know that these toxic feelings were conquered on the cross—the place where He paid it all for us.

Challenge: There are three steps we can take to rid ourselves of guilt. We should:

1. **Repent instead of rationalize.** We need to avoid wasting time making excuses for the actions that led to our guilt. The actions cannot be reversed and the feeling still remains. Use that time more productively by repenting and asking the Lord for forgiveness.

2. **Be responsible instead of blaming.** Projecting blame on others is another way we tend to make ourselves feel better about our guilt. We need to confess that *we* are responsible for behaving against God's will.

3. **Heal instead of hide.** We cannot set our guilt aside and deal with it another time. God is calling us to address our guilt *today* so that we can begin to heal with the new, clear conscience that He gives us. Postponing will not make the problem disappear.

What Satan whispers about guilt:

"God knows what you did and he will not accept you."

"Other people would be disgusted if they knew your struggle."

"There is no hope for your salvation after what you did."

What God whispers about guilt:

> *"There is therefore now no condemnation for those who are in Christ Jesus" (Romans 8:1).*

> *"For all have sinned and come short of the glory of God" (Romans 3:23).*

> *"My little children, I am writing these things to you so that you may not sin. But if anyone does sin, we*

have an advocate with the Father, Jesus Christ the righteous" (1 John 2:1).

Food for thought: In what ways have you noticed guilt consuming your life lately?

Prayer for us: Precious Savior, You are amazing. You had a plan from the very beginning to bless us with abundant lives. You knew we would be discouraged with guilt and negative feelings and that we could not deal with sin on our own. Thank You so much for sending Jesus to die on the cross to pay a debt we could never pay. We desire a clear conscience, but we need Your help. Free us from the guilt that is stifling us and the sin that separates us from You. We lift up this prayer in Your name—Amen.

HEALING

"I have to have a daily, vibrant relationship with Jesus in order to survive that process toward healing." —Beth Moore

As long as humankind exists on this earth, there will always be those of us who need healing. Many of us deal with physical, emotional, mental, and/or spiritual infirmities that put us into survival mode—just barely making it through the days. Physically, we are plagued with disabilities, chronic illnesses, and other attacks to our bodies. Emotionally, we have to deal with loss, grief, and broken hearts. Mentally, we are faced with mental illnesses and addictions that stifle us. Spiritually, we battle against believing in God and staying connected to him.

People often question why God allows suffering in this world. When God created this world, all things were perfect. The book of Genesis shows us that each thing He created was good. However, upon the creation of Adam and Eve and their disobedience that followed, evil, sin, and suffering entered into the world.

God never promised in his Word that Christians would be immune to suffering. In fact, He tells us that we will suffer on this earth. The Bible was given to us as the answer to navigating the problems we experience in this world. The Lord has blessed us with scriptures for comfort and the promise of God's plan to bring us to a place where no healing is required: Heaven.

We can find several biblical examples of God healing people of various infirmities. He was responsible for physical healing—making the blind see, the lame walk, the barren have children. He healed the emotionally sick, like Ruth, who lost her husband and found strength through the Lord—resulting in a beautiful, new love story. He restored those with mental struggles like Job, who lost everything and became hopeless and depressed, followed by receiving 140 more years of life and blessings. He worked spiritual miracles by turning unbelievers like Paul into people who were eager and committed to spreading the Gospel. He can heal us today.

Healing does not always appear in the form of unfathomable miracles or instantaneous recovery. Instead, healing is often found in the small victories like the strength to get through another day or the ability to be positive in the midst of negative circumstances. It is a process that we can only persevere through with the help of our heavenly Father. When we begin to recognize healing as a process, the small blessings from the Lord do not go unnoticed.

If you are seeking healing today, be encouraged. As you continue to pray about what is plaguing you, the Lord is listening. He is working behind the scenes to give you the help you need, little by little. You are not strong enough to handle this struggle on your own, but the Lord is fighting with you.

Challenge:

Write down what ideal healing looks like in your situation. How might you need to change your perspective in order to see the smaller steps toward healing that God can give you in the process?

What Satan whispers about healing:

"You can't be sure that better days actually await."

"Jesus did not pay the price for what you're going through."

"There is no hope in your affliction."

What God whispers about healing:

"I have told you these things so that in Me you may have peace. In this world you may have trouble, but behold, I have overcome the world" (John 16:33).

"Surely he took up our pain and bore our suffering, yet we considered him punished by God, stricken

by him, and afflicted. But he was pierced for our transgressions, he was crushed for our iniquities; the punishment that brought us peace was on him, and by his wounds we are healed" (Isaiah 53:4–6).

"Many are the afflictions of the righteous, But the Lord delivers him out of them all" (Psalm 34:19).

Food for thought: One helpful step to recovery is deciding to encourage someone else. Perhaps there is someone in your life that you can help along their healing process as the Lord helps you on yours.

Prayer for us: Heavenly Father, we thank You for the opportunity to sit in Your presence. We are on a difficult road and the days are rough. Lord, You have already overcome the suffering in this world. We praise You for the perfect place that awaits us if we follow Your will. Remind us that this life is but a vapor so that we can focus our hope on Heaven and not our present circumstances. Help us to not overlook the small ways You are giving us healing each day. In Your name we pray—Amen.

HOPELESSNESS

"Hope never abandons you, you abandon it." —
George Weinberg

Life is an ocean. We step carefully into the shallow waters of life, able to see everything before us—the beautiful treasures, as well as the areas of caution. As we continue on, trials come our way. The waves of doubt and hardship crash over us, and we somehow manage to come out with our heads above water. Just as soon as we conquer a wave we did not think we would make it through, a fiercer one crashes over us. The deep waters of tribulation begin to drown our positivity and hope. We become exhausted and lose purpose, allowing the current to carry us in the direction it would have us go.

Finding hope is a choice—a conscious decision we can make in the midst of feeling overwhelmed. Scientists have identified nine causes of the hopelessness that human beings experience. Fortunately, the Bible gives us encouragement to help us weather the storms of each category of hopelessness.

1. **Alienation**—Do you feel different and misunderstood? This alienation leads us to feel unworthy and close ourselves off out of fear of further pain and rejection. Do not allow your hope to be contingent upon others. As long as we put our hope and trust in human beings, we will continue to feel alienated. We have a God who understands us and is waiting for us to find hope in Him. *"Happy is he who has the God of Jacob for his help, whose hope is in the Lord his God" (Psalm 146:5).*

2. **Forsakenness**—Are you feeling totally abandoned in your time of need (like Job) and believing that nobody cares about you? God tells us in Hebrews 13:5, *"Never will I leave you, never will I forsake you."* He also reminds us that, *"When you go through deep waters, I will be with you" (Isaiah 43:2).* When everyone you love abandons you, God will still be there. He is the only constant.

3. **Uninspired**—Do you feel defeated because you lack the resources to pursue your goals? God knows what you need and is waiting for you to pray diligently instead of becoming discouraged. He tells us, *"Seek ye first the kingdom of God and his righteousness and all these things will be added unto you" (Matthew 6:33).* There is no need that He cannot supply. *"And my God will supply every need of yours, according to his riches in glory in Christ Jesus" (Philippians 4:19).*

4. **Powerlessness**—Have you been feeling as though you have no authority over the direction of your life? We must remember that taking our lives into our own hands is not wise. When we put our lives in His hands, we will never be led astray. *"A man's heart plans his way, but the Lord directs his steps" (Proverbs 16:9).* Stop feeling the need to control your life and give it over to the all-powerful, all-knowing God.

5. **Oppression**—You may be feeling downtrodden and crushed with no way out. Although the path seems bleak, the Lord is by your side in your oppression. *"The Lord will also be a refuge for the oppressed, a refuge in times of trouble" (Psalm 9:9).*

6. **Limitedness**—Perhaps you have been feeling as though you do not have what it takes to make it in the world. Be encouraged! The Lord has everything we need. *"The Lord is my rock and my fortress and my deliverer, my God, my rock, in whom I take refuge, my shield, and the hold of my salvation, my stronghold" (Psalm 18:2).*

7. **Doom**—Maybe you cannot live abundantly because you are in despair. You think that your life is essentially over and death is imminent. God reminds us that as Christians, we have strength to overcome any feelings of doom. *"We are*

hard-pressed on every side, yet not crushed; we are per-plexed, but not in despair; persecuted, but not forsaken; struck down but not destroyed" (2 Corinthians 4:8–9).

8. **Physical and Emotional Captivity**—Do you feel trapped in an unhealthy relationship or situation that is stealing your joy? We can become hopeless when we are in people bondage, constantly manipulated by others. God orders us to break free from these type of strongholds that lead to destruction rather than prosperity. *"A healthy tree cannot bear bad fruit, nor can a diseased tree bear good fruit. Every tree that does not bear good fruit is cut down and thrown into the fire" (Matthew 7:19).*

9. **Helplessness**—It might be the case that you feel as though you cannot live safely in this world, due to your vulnerability. God tells us that His grace and power has us covered! *"My grace is sufficient for you, for my power is made perfect in weakness" (2 Corinthians 12:9).*

God's word has held the answers to psychological concepts long before they were identified. The Bible tells us *"there is nothing new under the sun" (Ecclesiastes 1:9).* Trust the directions that God gives us in the scriptures. They have worked for the hopeless who truly believe since the beginning of time.

Challenge: From the nine examples given above, identify the cause of your hopelessness? Now that you know what may be spurring these feelings, make a personal plan for how to combat the root of the problem.

What Satan whispers about hopelessness:
"Why should you continue when there is no hope moving forward?"

"Where can you possibly find hope in your condition?"

"Your hopelessness is a sign of your weakness."

What God whispers about hopelessness:

> *"For I know the plans I have for you, plans to prosper*
> *you not harm you, plans to give you hope and a*
> *future" (Jeremiah 29:11).*

> *"May the God of hope fill you with all joy and peace*
> *in believing, so that by the power of the Holy Spirit*
> *you may abound in hope" (Romans 15:13).*

> *"For the sake of Christ, then, I am content with weak-*
> *nesses, insults, in hardships, in persecutions, in dif-*
> *ficulties. For when I am weak, then I am strong" (2*
> *Corinthians 12:10).*

Food for thought: Hopelessness is one of the early signs of depression. If you have been feeling hopeless for an extended amount of time, consider seeking help from a professional.

Prayer for us: Dear God, You are so faithful. Your word provides the encouragement we need for each of life's problems. Help us to remember that we are not alone when we go through deep waters. Give us the strength we need to find the hope to persevere. We need You now more than ever. We believe in Your power and declare that You will transform our situation. In Jesus' name—Amen.

HUMILITY

"Nothing is more deceitful than the appearance of humility. It is often only carelessness of opinion, and sometimes an indirect boast." —Jane Austen

P ride is one of Satan's sneakiest schemes to separate us from God. Even for people who shy away from the spotlight, the flesh naturally thrives on compliments, pats on the back, and approval from others. Life is good when we feel like we've got it all figured out. In the midst of trying to appear to have it all together, we sometimes begin to rely on our own abilities and wisdom more than the Lord's. We cannot afford to do life without our Savior. There are three areas that we can improve in order to remain humble women.

1. We need to humble ourselves in our daily prayers.

Humbling ourselves in prayer requires being transparent with God. He already knows our flaws, our insecurities, and our weaknesses. *"O Lord, you have searched me and know me"* Psalm 139:1. He knows the words on our tongues, the thoughts in our heads, and the ugliness in our hearts before we say or do anything. God is not looking for actresses. He is not entertained by our role playing the perfect, Christian woman when we come to Him in prayer. Doing so can make us grow complacent in our Christian walks, feeling as though we are doing enough for the Lord. No matter how much we study our bibles, how many times a day we pray, how many ways we serve at church, how many sinful activities we avoid–there is *always* room for growth. He wants us to come to Him as the broken sinners that we are; desperate for Him. Furthermore, He knows when our prayers are not genuine. He is fully aware when we are praying with selfish intent, seeking for Him to answer in the way that we want instead of truly submitting to His will.

2. We need to humble ourselves in our daily accomplishments.
Our existence and accomplishments are meaningless without God. We work hard and become proud when we see the fruits of our labor—getting promotions at work, raising accomplished children, making good grades on assignments, keeping a happy husband, and the list goes on. Our education, talents, good deeds, good looks, and hard work are not what earns us God's favor. James 1:17 tells us that, *"every good and perfect gift is from above."* We cannot forget that our blessings are because of God's doing, not our doing.

3. We need to humble ourselves in our daily interactions with others.
For some of us, pride can be an issue when we interact with our friends, family, and coworkers. We have difficulty admitting when we are wrong or make mistakes. We are stubborn in clinging to our justifications and rationales. This is a dangerous habit. Our humility can never fully develop until we are able to take a step back and learn from other people.

Challenge: Write down and reflect on the following things:
- What would being more humble look like in your life?
- If you were able to achieve the humility you desire, who would notice? What would they notice about you?

What Satan whispers about your pride:
"God doesn't mind if you give yourself the credit- you worked hard."
"It's okay to want the world to know you are confident by showing how awesome you are."
"You don't have to budge. Show them that your decision is always the right decision."

What God whispers about your pride:

> *"He resists the proud, but gives grace to the humble"*
> *(James 4:6).*

> *"For by the grace given to me I say to everyone*
> *among you not to think of himself more highly than*
> *he ought to think, but to think with sober judgment,*
> *each according to the measure of faith that God has*
> *assigned" (Romans 12:3).*

> *"When pride comes, then comes disgrace, but with*
> *the humble is wisdom" (Proverbs 11:2).*

Food for thought: Which area of showing humility are you currently struggling with the most?

Prayer for us: Dear God, we humbly approach You. We are broken and sinful, and we cannot make it through each day without You. We know that all blessings come from above. Help us to be humble in our daily walks. Help us not to take credit for our blessings, but rather give You glory. We want to be examples of humility in all that we do, so that others can see Jesus in us. We ask these things in Your name—Amen.

INADEQUACY

"We enslave in the manner we talk to ourselves. But the truth is, God already set us free. He secured our release. To constantly hurt ourselves, resting in our inadequacy, is to call Him a LIAR." —Mary E. DeMuth

Expectations can be a blessing and a curse. They can help us to avoid growing complacent; however, they can also lead us to be discontent and diminish our confidence. Sometimes, our inadequacy results from feeling as though we are not living up to the expectations others have for us—parents, bosses, spouses, children, or friends. More often than not, our feelings of inadequacy are the result of self-imposed expectations.

As long as we are trying to compete with the standards of the world, we will feel inadequate. There will always be a smarter, prettier, more creative woman. There will always be a better daughter, better girlfriend, better wife, and a better mom. There will always be somebody that is praying more, serving more, loving more. We have to rid ourselves of social comparison. When we compare our performance to others, we are making them our standard, rather than Jesus Christ. That is called *an idol*. Ouch.

Dear Sister, the formula to feeling adequate is no secret. The formula is to find worth and adequacy in your identity in Christ. A life in Christ levels the playing field. There is no ranking or hierarchy for people who are the best. There is no special reward that God gives to recognize a "super Christian." We all come to Him—equally broken and full of sin, needing him every step of the way. If we are living according to His will, we will receive an equal reward—eternal life.

> *"For am I now seeking the approval of man, or of God? Or am I trying to please man? If I were still trying to please man, I would not be a servant of Christ" (Galatians 1:10).*

Imagine that you bought a gift for one of your dearest friends that you knew she could never purchase herself. You bought it out of the goodness of your heart, because you knew that this gift would bring her so much joy and happiness. After you give her the gift, she expresses her gratitude. She is so pleased and excited over it—until a week later when she seemingly forgets about it. Something else has caught her attention and now she is not even enjoying the free gift that she received from you. You would feel pretty crushed and unappreciated, huh?

This is probably how God feels when we sulk in our inadequacies. He paid the ultimate price for us to live abundantly, because He knew that we could not do it on our own. He tells us in the Bible that His grace is sufficient for us (2 Corinthians 12:9). He reminds us that we are more precious than rubies (Proverbs 3:15) and that we are worthy. We know these truths and we boast these truths regularly, but when it comes to our daily walks, oh how quickly we forget! We are adequate because we have the Lord. What an insult to our Savior— to not take advantage of the peace that He has freely provided for us but rather choose to be in bondage to inadequacy.

Challenge: Make a list of all of your personal strengths (talents, personal attributes, etc.). Looking at these strengths, how can you use what God has already blessed you with to pursue your purpose? Say a prayer of praise to the Lord for the unique strengths he has given you.

What Satan whispers about inadequacy:
"Your weaknesses will limit you from measuring up."
"You are worthless."
"Inadequacy doesn't separate you from God."

What God whispers about inadequacy:

> *"My grace is sufficient for you, for my strength is made perfect in weakness" (2 Corinthians 12:9).*

> *"She is more precious than jewels, and nothing you desire can compare to her" (Proverbs 3:15).*

> *"Let us then approach the throne of grace with confidence, so that we may receive mercy and find grace to help us in our time of need" (Hebrews 4:16).*

Food for thought: What are your inadequacies stopping you from doing? How are they separating you from Christ?

Prayer for us: Dear Lord, we thank You for all of Your blessings. You are all that we need to be adequate in this world. You paid a price that we could have never paid alone. Help us to never take that peace for granted. We want to stop trying to measure up to the standards of this world and live for You. Give us the guidance we need to focus on the strengths You have blessed us with—and help us to use these things for Your glory. In Your name we declare these things—Amen.

Glimmers of Hope

JOY

———)❧(———

"Participate joyfully in the sorrows of the world. We cannot cure the world of sorrows, but we can choose to live in joy." —Joseph Campbell

God created us with the unique ability to experience multiple emotions simultaneously. When things are going well, we find ourselves a little sorrowful that the blissful, carefree moments cannot last forever. Likewise, when life brings sorrow our way, we can find joy in knowing that better days await us.

Some people argue that Christians should always be happy. Happiness is fleeting and can be shattered when a trial or test of faith comes our way. Being Christians does not make us invincible. We are not immune to feelings of grief or sorrow. A Christian should not always be happy, but a Christian should be joyful in all circumstances.

Joy is more about choosing to recognize God's hand in every situation and place. It is knowing that our undesired life interruptions are divine interventions. It is being able to count the small blessings in front of us, even when the number of things going well seem sparse.

Although we often hear that joy is a choice, it is actually a commandment for Christians to live by. Philippians 4:4 says, *"Rejoice in the Lord always; again, I will say, rejoice!"* This statement was made by the apostle Paul—someone who had every reason to not choose joy in the midst of his bleak circumstances. In the book of Acts, we learn that Paul and Silas were thrown into prison—persecuted for spreading the Gospel of Jesus Christ. They were stripped

91

naked, beaten with rods, and charged. Then the very next verse tells us that they were singing hymns and praying. That's right—they were *rejoicing*. There was not a scripture in between that said they whined or complained. There was no scripture that said they were discouraged and shook a fist at God. They found their strength and joy in the Lord, regardless of being victimized and mistreated.

What would our lives be like if we chose joy in all circumstances? If we prayed our way through our lives' storms instead of complaining about them? If we went around singing hymns and praising God when we feel enslaved to our unfortunate situations? If we fail to find joy in anything else, we should find it in the fact we have salvation through Jesus Christ. This should be the ultimate source of joy for believers!

Challenge:
- Take a moment to count some of your blessings. Write down five things that you have to rejoice in today.
- In what ways do you see the hand of the Lord at work in your life right now?

What Satan whispers about joy:
"You are at a low point. How can you possibly find joy?"
"God is not concerned with giving you joy."
"You don't have to rejoice. God doesn't care if you choose not to."

What God whispers about joy:

"Consider all joy, my brethren, when you encounter various trials, knowing that the testing of your faith produces endurance" (James 1:2–3).

"You make known to me the path of life; in Your presence is fullness of joy; at your right hand are pleasures forevermore" (Psalm 16:11).

"Rejoice in hope, be patient in tribulation, be constant in prayer" (Romans 12:12).

Food for thought: In what ways have you been allowing Satan to steal your joy lately? When he feeds you lies, fight back with God's word!

Prayer for us: Our Lord and Savior, You are the ultimate source of joy. You give us the joy of knowing we have salvation through You. Thank You for reminding us to rejoice in all things and situations. God, we are struggling. Rejoicing during our dark days is easier said than done. Help us to find the strength to fight back when the enemy tries to steal our joy. Help us to praise You continually and see Your hand at work in our lives. In Your name we pray—Amen.

LETTING GO

"Some of us think holding on makes us strong, but sometimes it is letting go." —Hermann Hesse

Picking foreign objects off the ground and carrying them around is a favorite pastime of every kid at some point during early childhood. It is always the same story but with different objects. Child sees thing on the ground. Child picks thing up. Child carries thing around (and sometimes attempts to eat it). Adult intercedes and takes object away to protect child. And then comes the meltdown! The child fights, kicks, and screams trying to get that thing back— followed by a bad attitude with whichever grown up took the toy away to protect them.

As adults, it is intriguing how often our behavior mimics the scenario above. We absolutely despise letting go of things that we treasure. Sometimes it is a job we love. Other times it is a relationship or friendship. It might even be a certain place or location. It is always the same story but a different thing. God decides that it is not the right thing for us. He calls us to let it go and BAM! Here comes the meltdown. We whine, we cry, we complain. We bargain with God. And when He still doesn't give it back, we resent Him. We prefer holding on to our desires, rather than His hand of protection.

What makes letting go so difficult is our limited perspective of our lives. God sees the full picture, while we only see pixel by tiny pixel. Like a child, we feel punished and deprived when He leads us to let go. But like any good Father would, He protects His children.

John 15:2 tells us, *"Every branch in me that does not bear fruit he takes away, and every branch that does bear fruit he prunes, that it may bear more fruit."* Dear sister, there is something about the situation He is calling you to leave that is not in your best interest. I know you cannot see it now, but that person, place, or thing does not profit you. We have to trust that even when we are certain of what we want, God is the only one who knows what we need. When He calls us to let go, it is to prevent the future struggle, pain, and heartache that is only visible to Him.

Don't resist God's perfect route and detour to the long, rocky roads of your own understanding. Stop holding on reluctantly. You can't reach out and grasp the new, good thing He has waiting for you if your hands are not free.

Challenge:

Write a short journal entry to answer these three questions:

1. Do I trust God when He is asking me to let this (person, thing, job, etc.) go?
2. Why am I hesitant to give it up?
3. Can I live without it?

What Satan whispers about letting go:

"The thing God is calling you to let go of is too precious."

"You cannot trust that God telling you to let go is the right thing to do."

"You can make your own decision to hold on and still be okay in the future."

What God whispers about letting go:

"Brothers and Sisters, I do not consider myself yet to have taken hold of it. But one thing I do: Forgetting what is behind and straining toward what is ahead, I press on toward the goal to win the prize for which God has called me heavenward in Christ Jesus" (Philippians 3:14).

*"Oh the depth, of the riches and wisdom and knowl-
edge of God! How unsearchable are His judgements
and how inscrutable His ways" (Romans 11:33).*

*"I am the vine; you are the branches. Whoever abides
in me and I in him; he it is that bears much fruit, for
apart from me you can do nothing" (John 15:5).*

Food for thought: Think of a time in the past when God required
you to let something go. What were your initial thoughts? What did
you end up learning?

Prayer for us: Dear Lord, we humbly approach You. You are the
Vine and we are the branches. We know that we cannot do anything
without You. You know exactly what is good for us and which parts
of our life are not going to bear fruit. Help us to trust You when You
ask us to let go. Help us to believe that You have something better
in store, if only we obey. We trust in Your word and wisdom. These
things we ask in Your name—Amen.

LONELINESS

*"Loneliness and the feeling of being unwanted is the
most terrible poverty."* —Mother Teresa

Feeling as though we are walking through this life alone is a terribly frightening, isolating experience. Maybe you are a lonely single, feeling that God will never grant you companionship. Or perhaps you are a lonely spouse, feeling distant from the man you gave your heart and vows to. You could be a lonely survivor of a dear loved one who has passed away. Or a lonely sufferer, feeling as though nobody can relate to the illness you are enduring. Some of you may even be lonely servants of God, cut off from the people you love because of your decision to be a follower of Christ.

In the moments that we feel most alone, Christ is calling us to draw nearer to Him. In fact, sometimes being alone is necessary to hear the Lord's voice and seeking His discernment. Let us consider an experience in which Jesus isolated Himself. The Holy Spirit led Him to the wilderness to pray. For forty days and forty nights, our Lord was apart from friends and family. He was distanced from all people and all things, yet in the presence of God—relying on Him for strength and guidance.

Loneliness does not only happen when we are physically alone. Sometimes, there are an abundance of people around us, but we still feel that our experience is unique and misunderstood. It is okay and natural to feel lonely at times. But danger arises when we begin to allow our loneliness to consume us. Satan tries to win us over, by leading our loneliness to transpire into self-pity.

Challenge:
There are three things we must do to ensure that our loneliness does not lead us into a downward spiral of emotions:
1. **Acknowledge that you are lonely.** You cannot address loneliness until you admit that it is an issue. Being unashamed to express these feelings has to be the first step.
2. **Draw nearer to Christ.** If you are struggling with feelings of loneliness (especially physical loneliness), you are in the perfect position to spend time with the Lord, distraction-free. When you recognize that He is all that you need, His presence becomes enough.
3. **Connect with other believers.** You may be feeling as if nobody understands your personal struggle. Getting connected to a network of other Christians can be a wonderful remedy. While they may not relate to your loneliness, they can pray for you and encourage you in these dark moments. Matthew 18:20 tells us, *"For where two or three are gathered in my name, there am I with them."* Spending time with other believers will help you draw nearer to Christ. Your brothers and sisters in Christ can pray for you when it seems hard to find the strength to pray for yourself.

What Satan whispers about loneliness:
"Everyone abandoned you."
"God has forgotten about you."
"You are alone in your darkness."

What God whispers about loneliness:

"At my first defense, no one came to stand by me but all deserted me. May it not be charged against them! But the Lord stood by me and strengthened me" (2 Timothy 4:16, 17).

"And surely I am with you always, to the very end of the age" (Matthew 28:20).

"Do not be afraid, for I am with you" (Isaiah 43:5).

Food for thought: Are you running to the Lord in prayer each time feelings of loneliness come over you? Or are you suffering silently?

Prayer for us: Father God, You are faithful. In our darkest moments, You will never forsake us. When we have no other companion, we have access to You 24/7, through prayer. Thank You for being there for us in every season. We need Your help when Satan causes our loneliness to make us feel overwhelmed and isolated. Please help us to lean on other believers and lean on You. In Your name we declare these things—Amen.

Glimmers of Hope

LUST

—)❦(—

*"Lusts are the cords with which Satan binds men; our
fiery trials are God's messengers sent to loose these
bands."* —A. Ritchie

E very second of the day, we are in spiritual warfare. There is
a battle that rages within us, between our flesh and our spirit.
The Bible gives us a detailed picture of how the two work within us.

*"The acts of the flesh are obvious: sexual immorality,
impurity and debauchery; idolatry and witchcraft;
hatred, discord, jealousy, fits of rage, selfish ambi-
tion, dissensions, factions and envy; drunkenness,
orgies, and the like. I warn you, as I did before, that
those who live like this will not inherit the kingdom
of God. But the fruit of the Spirit is love, joy, peace,
forbearance, kindness, goodness, faithfulness, gen-
tleness and self-control. Against such things there is
no law. Those who belong to Christ Jesus have crucified the flesh with its passions and desires. Since
we live by the Spirit, let us keep in step with the
Spirit"* (Galatians 5:19–25).

Our flesh would love to take us on a joy ride through this life,
giving way to every desire for the thrill of it. The flesh wants to dictate all of our senses and lure us down forbidden paths—spending
our money impulsively, eating and drinking the things we know we

should abstain from, indulging in sexual sin (mentally or physically), gossiping about other women, and many other carnal desires. Our flesh screams, "This life is about enjoying yourself!"

Our spirit wants us to remember that this life is about glorifying the Lord. We were created to worship Him. Our existence and everything we do should be to bring Him the glory He so rightfully deserves. When the battle begins and the tests come our way, we have to be ready to fight back. Are you ready for war, dear sister?

Challenge:

Consider using these guidelines to overcome lust and whatever fleshly desires you are struggling with:

1. **Frequent "heart checks."** Sin begins in the heart. James 1:15 tells us, *"Then desire when it has conceived, gives birth to sin, and sin when it is fully grown brings forth death."* We need to make sure that we are not overlooking the sin that is within us. Just because we are not acting on it, does not mean we are not desiring it. We should pray frequently for God to survey our hearts and show us our unclean ways.

2. **Rebuke Satan.** When the enemy brings lust to your heart, scare him away with God's truths. *"Submit yourselves therefore to God. Resist the devil and he will flee from you" (James 4:7).* The Gospel is the only thing that will make Satan flee. It is more powerful than any of his temptations. Furthermore, remember that fleeing from sin is a conscious decision you can make. 1 Corinthians 10:13 says, *"No temptation has overtaken you that is not common to man. God is faithful, and he will not let you be tempted beyond your ability, but with the temptation he will also provide the way of escape, that you may be able to endure it."*

3. **Reframe your thoughts.** When lustful thoughts come to our minds, we need to refocus our attention on spiritual things. Do not allow the thoughts of the flesh to simmer and turn into an act of sin. What positive thoughts can we use to replace the sinful thoughts? Philippians 4:8 gives us a detailed list: *"Finally, brothers, whatever is true, whatever is honorable, whatever is just, whatever is pure, whatever is lovely, whatever is commendable, if there is any excellence, if there is*

anything worthy of praise, think about these things." Stop meditating on trash TV, social media, and vulgar music. These things can be replaced by the truths that give us the fuel we need in our Christian walk.

What Satan whispers about lust:
"You have to have fun while you can. A few bad decisions make for good stories."
"God created these things so you could enjoy them. Take advantage of it."
"It's your life and your body. You can do whatever you want."

What God whispers about lust:

"Flee the evil desires of youth and pursue righteousness, faith, love, and peace, along with those who call on the Lord out of a pure heart" (2 Timothy 2:22).

"For everything in the world—the lust of the flesh, the lust of the eyes, and the pride of life—comes not from the Father but from the world" (1 John 2:16).

"Therefore, I urge you, brothers and sisters, in view of God's mercy, to offer your bodies as a living sacrifice, holy and pleasing to God—this is your true and proper worship. Do not conform to the pattern of this world, but be transformed by the renewing of your mind. Then you will be able to test and approve what God's will is—his good, pleasing and perfect will" (Romans 12:1–2).

Food for thought: If you had to consider whether your flesh or your spirit is dictating more of your life right now, which would it be? Make a list of the temptations you want to flee and how you plan to do it.

Prayer for us: God, we come to You right now as imperfect sinners. You are faithful to us in the midst of our sinful lives. You show us unending love and amazing grace and mercy. We want to glorify

You and honor You with our lives and our bodies. We declare that
Satan will not have power over our hearts. We know that You never
leave us without an escape from temptation. Help us to meditate on
Your truths and fight back when the tests come. In Your name we ask
these things—Amen!

MEDITATION

"Meditation is the ultimate mobile device. You can use it anywhere, anytime, unobtrusively." —Sharon Salzberg

All of us have been guilty of "busy-body syndrome" at some point or another. We run here and run there—cleaning the house, working on projects, running kids to their destinations, attending meetings, cooking, working out, grocery shopping, serving at church, and the list goes on! The days seem long and the hours we have to work with seem short. Suddenly, finding balance seems like an impossible task.

Meditation has become a popular remedy for many women who desire to obtain the clarity and peace of mind that seems so out of reach. Several studies have shown the physical and psychological benefits of meditation, including (but not limited to) decreased stress and tension-related pain, improved immune system, lower blood pressure, increased serotonin for mood and behavior, and more energy. There is no doubt that consistently practicing meditation can improve our lifestyle.

The concept of mediation is more than just a research-based suggestion. It is a practice that God intended for us to participate in, as revealed in His word. Psalm 46:10 tells us, *"Be still and know that I am God."* Our Lord knows more about what we need than any doctor or scientist. He created us and He knows our struggle to be still before Him. He recognizes that we like to have control. He watches us attempt to multitask like superwomen and burnout, because we are not adequately fueled with His presence.

"Oh how I love your law! It is my meditation all the day. Your commandment makes me wiser than my enemies, for it is ever with me. I have more understanding than all my teachers, for your testimonies are my meditation" (Psalm 119:97–99).

When we meditate on God's word, we receive the strength and wisdom we need to make it through each day, living according to His glory. We gain discernment to help us make godly decisions. And we acquire the tools to help us fix our minds on Jesus when Satan tries to break us.

But what does it look like to meditate on the Word? Meditating on the word goes beyond reading a few scriptures. We have to be intentional in order for meditation to be effective. It is walking, talking, and acting in alignment with God's truths. First, we should consider what aspect of our spiritual life we are struggling with the most. Then, we should study the scriptures and stories in the Bible that are relevant to that issue. As we read, we must make practical applications to our lives. In addition, we should consider writing the scriptures down in a place where we can easily revisit them. Be still, my sister. Breathe. Keep perspective. Immerse yourself in the Word. Release your cares to our Lord.

Challenge:

- Imagine there was a scale from 1 to 10 for how well you are addressing your most difficult spiritual dilemma (1 = you are not doing well at all, 10 = you have overcome it). Where do you currently fall on this scale?
- On a notecard, write down a scripture (or scriptures) relevant to your spiritual dilemma. Carry this notecard in your purse or position it in a visible place (on your fridge, on your wall, in your office, on your laptop, etc.). Recite and pray over these words daily, to give you the fuel you need.
- One week later, rate yourself again to assess any improvements you have made on the scale. If you notice progress,

repeat this routine. If not, continue to work towards progress and spiritual growth. Remember: The process for every individual is different. Some spiritual dilemmas take longer to overcome than others and that is okay!

What Satan whispers about meditation:
"Meditating on God's word is a waste of your time."
"You don't have time to meditate, because you have more important things to do."
"Just reading a few scriptures is adequate."

What God whispers about meditation:

"This Book of the Law shall not depart from your mouth, but you shall meditate on it day and night, so that you may be careful to do according to all that is written in it. For then you will make your way prosperous, and then you will have good success" *(Joshua 1:8).*

"Be still, and know that I am God. I will be exalted among the nations, I will be exalted in the earth!" *(Psalm 46:10).*

"My son, be attentive to my words; incline your ear to my sayings. Let them not escape from your sight; keep them within your heart. For they are life to those who find them, and healing to all their flesh" *(Proverbs 4:20–22).*

Food for thought: What are some practical times you can study God's word, so that you will be able to meditate on what you have read? Write meditation time into your schedule or planner.

Prayer for us: Our Father in Heaven, we are taking a moment to breathe deeply and sit before You. You are the provider of peace. You remind us of the importance of meditating on Your statutes. Help us to prioritize You, in the midst of our busy schedules. Fill us up with Your word and bind it to our hearts. In Your name we pray—Amen.

NEW BEGINNINGS

"Every new beginning comes from some other beginning's end." —Seneca

Just as sure as a door opens, it can close. Our lives are the sum of the opening and closing of many doors—jobs, relationships, seasons of life, places, and opportunities. Sometimes, a door closes as a result of our own will. We make the choice to embrace a new thing. Other times, God closes a door without our input. We are forced to adjust accordingly (often reluctantly). And somehow in both cases, there is a fear that lingers in the unknown of a new beginning.

Adjustments are difficult, because we are creatures of habit. We gravitate toward anything that elicits consistency and stability. So we tend to tiptoe in hesitation toward new beginnings, even when they are our choice. "This will either be more awesome than I can imagine right now or a step toward imminent disaster," we think.

If your new beginning flew at you like a meteor—scary, unwanted, abrupt—there are a few things to remember. The Lord may be pushing you toward this new beginning, but He is not doing it without purpose, and you are not alone.

"Behold, I am doing a new thing; now it springs forth, do you not perceive it? I will make a way in the wilderness and rivers in the desert" (Isaiah 43:19).

God is doing a new thing in your life and He so desperately wants you to recognize it. If it feels as though He has led you into the wilderness, don't be so quick to escape. There are lessons to be learned in this unfamiliar territory. And God is going to keep you there until you embrace it. You will have to go through the process, eventually—no matter how much you kick your feet. So what will your attitude be as you walk through this new door? Remember, a door may be closed but not locked. Your prayer may be delayed but not denied. Your story may be paused but not concluded.

If your new beginning is something you desired—a new love, a new job, marriage, motherhood—rejoice! God is ready to use you in tremendous ways. Do not fear the fact that you lack answers. Do not feel as though you have to be perfect in this new place or position. Seek Christ and He will guide you, just as He has all along.

> *"Seek ye first the kingdom of God and His righteousness; and all these things shall be added unto you"* *(Matthew 6:33).*

Challenge: List the exciting possibilities that God might be pushing you toward in this new season of your life. (Don't be afraid to dream big when you are listing the possibilities. Have faith, because we serve a God who is able!) Say a prayer that God will help you to approach this new season boldly, with the confidence that He will guide you.

What Satan whispers about new beginnings:
"What if disaster awaits in this new beginning?"
"What if what you are leaving behind is better than what is ahead?"
"You need to proceed with caution to guard yourself."

What God whispers about new beginnings:

> *"For I know the plans I have for you,"* declares the Lord, *"plans to prosper you and not to harm you, plans to give you hope and a future" (Jeremiah 29:11).*

> *"Now to him who is able to do immeasurably more than all we ask or imagine, according to his power that is at work within us" (Ephesians 3:20).*

"For the Spirit God gave us does not make us timid, but gives us power, love, and self-discipline" (2 Timothy 1:7).

Food for thought: Has God closed a door before and allowed you to see the greater good, down the road? What are some ways He has been faithful to you, in the past?

Prayer for us: Our loving Father in Heaven, We sit at your feet in this new beginning. Help us to approach this new beginning with confidence and positivity. You would not bring us to it if You could not bring us through it. Help us to remember that the plans You have for us are good. And please help us to learn the lessons we need to, along the way. You will never abandon us and we declare You are with us always. In Your name we pray—Amen.

OBEDIENCE

"One act of obedience is better than one hundred sermons." —Dietrich Bonhoeffer

We have all worn the shoes of disobedience. An authority figure instructs us to do something, we take it with a grain of salt, and do the opposite. Nearly as bad is being the one who instructs a person to do something and then watching them disregard your instruction and suffer the consequences. Lack of obedience results in regret. Although lessons are learned, we recognize that the path would have been much smoother if the road of wise instruction was taken.

I imagine God cringing at our disobedience. He gives us His word—a whole rule book of instruction. He provides us with signs and instincts to caution us when we are going in the wrong direction. He tries to reroute us when we have made a wrong turn—yet we continuously travel the winding, unpaved road of our stubborn will.

"Why do you call me, 'Lord, Lord,' and do not do what I say?" (Luke 6:46).

Our obedience—or lack thereof—speaks volume about our love for God. We use all the Christian phrases to express our love for Him. We tell others how blessed we are to be His children and to be set apart. But when it is time to obey His commandments, we suddenly become wiser than our Lord. Well, at least that is what our disobedience implies.

In general, we obey authority figures (like police officers) out of reverence and fear of consequences. But when we obey authority figures who we have *relationships* with (like parents and grandparents), *love* plays a major role in our actions. When we make the choice to obey, we please those who have instructed us. When we fail to obey, we disappoint them. Likewise, God is celebrating with us when we follow His commandments. But He is terribly grieved when we choose disobedience.

> *"And do not grieve the Holy Spirit of God, by whom you were sealed for the day of redemption" (Ephesians 4:30).*

Let's consider one man in the Bible who suffered the consequences of his disobedience. The prophet Jonah was commanded by the Lord to go to the great city of Nineveh to preach against the wickedness occurring there. Jonah ran away from the Lord and his calling, and he headed to a city called Tarshish. He went down to Joppa, where he found a ship that was setting sail for Tarshish. So Jonah hopped on the ship to flee from the Lord. God sent a violent storm with raging winds on the sea. The sailors on the ship cried out to their individual gods as the storm raged, and what was Jonah doing? He was sleeping. As the frantic sailors cried out to save their lives, they awoke Jonah and directed him to call on his God—our Lord and Savior. When Jonah confessed to worshipping God, the sailors knew that he was the reason for the storm and turbulence. He disobeyed God and obviously caused wrath and a consequence for everyone. Jonah directed them to throw him overboard so that the storm would cease. They eventually cast him into the sea, where the Lord ordered a great fish to swallow him. There he sat, in the fish's belly for three days and three nights. The Lord commanded the fish to vomit Jonah out on to dry land. I'm sure Jonah would have loved if the turmoil ended there, but the voice of the Lord came to him again. "Go to Nineveh." And so Jonah went reluctantly where he was supposed to go all along.

Running from the Lord got Jonah nowhere, and the same applies to us today. What is God calling you to do that you are running from? Have you been disobedient in your daily walk? Or are you running away from an even bigger purpose that He has directed you toward? We cannot hide from our all-knowing, all-powerful God. In our attempt to flee from His will, we put ourselves right in the midst of danger. Even worse, our disobedience impacts the people around us. Because of Jonah's disobedience, an entire ship of other men had to suffer the turbulence. Who might be suffering as a result of your disobedience? Refusal to obey can put us into a dark and murky place, like the fish's belly. And even after we have come out, guess what? The mission still remains and God's command still awaits us! Let's save ourselves the trouble of being shaken, swallowed up, and spat out by this life. Let's choose to obey and act according to the will of God instead.

Challenge: Write a short reflection about a time that you disobeyed God.

- What were the consequences?
- What might the path have looked like if you would have chosen obedience?
- What steps are you taking to avoid making the mistake of being disobedient, again?

What Satan whispers about disobedience:

"Everyone else is telling you what you want to do is okay. So do what you feel is best."

"There are more pros than cons to doing things your way."

"Disobeying God a few times doesn't mean you don't love him."

What God whispers about disobedience:

> *"Let no one deceive you with empty words, for because of such things God's wrath comes on those who are disobedient" (Ephesians 5:6).*

> *"If you are willing and obedient, you will eat the good things of the land; but if you resist and rebel, you will be devoured by the sword. For the mouth of the LORD has spoken" (Isaiah 1:19–20).*

"If you love me, keep my commandments"
(John 14:15).

Food for thought: What obstacles are getting in the way of you obeying God? What are some practical ways you might remove those barriers?

Prayer for us: Dear God, You are the ruler of all things. You have given us commandments that are in our best interest and You want us to follow them. Thank You for Your patience with us when we disobey You. Help us to walk according to Your will, instead of running away from it. Help us to stop trying to figure out alternate routes that will lead us astray. We need help removing the barriers that deter us from obedience. We declare that You know what is best for us. In Your name we pray—Amen.

Glimmers of Hope

PATIENCE

*"Patience is not simply the ability to wait—it's how
we behave while we're waiting."* —Joyce Meyer

Waiting is typically the result of us not having another choice. We are placed into circumstances or seasons in our lives that are beyond our control. And so we wait—but how do we behave while we are waiting? Do we exude a true attitude of patience?

"God, where is my husband?"

"God, when will I become a mommy?"

"God, where is my breakthrough in my career?"

"God, when will I become a homeowner?"

"God, will I ever see the fruits of my labor?"

"God, you are taking too long!"

We become victims of destination addiction—a preoccupation that happiness will be found in the next person, next job, next place, next accomplishment. Destination addiction distracts us from focusing on the only destination that matters—Heaven. Seasons of drought are an inevitable part of our lives. In those moments, the things we are waiting for seem out of reach. As we go through our dry seasons, Satan knows we are vulnerable. He hears every complaint, every time we question God about how long we have to wait, every time we pray to rush through the drought. And he thrives off of our impatience—just waiting to win us over.

God is watching how we behave, during our dry season. He is waiting to bless us after this season of waiting, but we are not proving that we are equipped to handle the blessings that are in store. We fail the test of the waiting game when we are not truly grateful for the portion He has already given us. God's word shows us the benefits of trusting His timing for our lives.

"He is like a tree planted by streams of water that yields its fruit in its season, and its leaf does not wither. In all that he does, he prospers" (Psalm 1:3).

"They will be like a tree planted by the water that sends out its roots by the stream. It does not fear when heat comes; its leaves are always green. It has no worries in a year of drought and never fails to bear fruit" (Jeremiah 17:8).

"Everyone who drinks this water will be thirsty again, but whoever drinks the water I give them will never thirst. Indeed, the water I give them will become in them a spring of water welling up to eternal life" (John 4:13-14).

While in a drought, we need to behave boldly, recognizing that it is called a "season" for a reason. The circumstances will not last forever. If we thirst for righteousness rather than destinations, we will behave as though we lack nothing. We will be grateful and give praise for our portion. We will wait patiently as God allows us to bear fruit. And we will not allow impatience and lack of faith in God's timing to rob us of our hope and blessings.

"He has made everything beautiful in its time. Also, he has put eternity into man's heart, yet so that he cannot find out what God has done from the beginning to the end" (Ecclesiastes 3:11).

Challenge:
- Write down all of the thoughts you are having in your season of waiting.
- Looking at the list, do most of your thoughts exude a positive attitude toward waiting? Or a negative attitude?

- How can you change the negative thoughts you wrote down into positive thoughts?

What Satan whispers about patience:
"Waiting is taking much longer than expected. Just give up because it is not going to happen."
"How do you know your season of drought will ever end?"
"There is no hope in this."

What God whispers about patience:

> *"And let us not grow weary of doing good, for in due season we will reap, if we do not give up"* *(Galatians 6:9).*

> *"For still the vision awaits its appointed time; it hastens to the end—it will not lie. If it seems slow, wait for it; it will surely come; it will not delay"* *(Habakkuk 2:3).*

> *"But if we hope for what we do not yet have, we wait for it patiently" (Romans 8:25).*

Food for thought: As a Christian, you are a living picture of Christ. In your season of waiting, would the folks around you describe you as more focused on destination addiction or destination eternity?

Prayer for us: Dear Father, you are everything we need. You have created eternity with us in mind. Thank you for Your promises of the good things that await us. Help us to be thankful with our portion and to not grow weary as we wait for the next blessings that You have in store. We want to have good attitudes and be positive in our current seasons. We declare that You will make all things beautiful in *Your* time. These things we set at Your feet and ask in Your name—Amen.

PRAYER

*"There is not in the world a kind of life more sweet
and delightful than that of a continual conversation
with God."* —Brother Lawrence

A s Christians, we have been given the greatest gift in the world. How precious a gift it is—24/7 access to the Creator of the heavens, the earth, and humanity. Our Creator, the very One who formed us in the womb and is carrying us through this life, desires to be our best friend. He has given us prayer to use as a method of venting, opportunity for His intercession, restoration of hope, and weapon against the enemy.

Take a moment to consider how much you treasure sweet moments with your friends and family. How you wish the moments of loving them and bonding with could last forever. How it is so hard to say goodbye and you long for the next time you can be in their presence. How you associate them with freedom, relaxation, and peace.

This is exactly the way our prayer life should be. We should treasure the moments when we can escape to converse with our Father, sitting at His feet in humble adoration. We should wish that our conversations with Him could be never ending. We should dread the moment that we have to leave His presence. We should associate our intimate prayer time with relief, rejuvenation, and peace of mind.

I often hear people express their desire for a more abundant prayer life. There is no secret formula to a "perfect prayer life." As you seek the Lord with all your heart, soul, and mind, prayer will become a natural desire. Like a car with no gas, you will feel empty without it—barely making your way. But just as most of us have had a few times where we let our cars get low on gas, sometimes we inadvertently neglect our prayer life, until the fear of breaking down is imminent.

Here are three common mistakes we make when it comes to our prayer life:

1. **Praying inconsistently.** Sometimes we treat calling on God like calling 911. When things are going fine and dandy, we let the good times roll! Sure, we know God is present and we are thankful for His faithfulness, but we do not feel the need to pray fervently. But as soon as a personal emergency happens, we call on God and expect Him to come to our aid, immediately! This is the wrong attitude to have. Do you like friends who only call you when they need something? Or do you cherish the friends who share the good stuff with you, too? The friends who want you to be a part of the good and the bad? 1 Thessalonians 5:17 directs us to, *"Pray without ceasing."* Our relationship with God should not be conditional. Do not make the mistake of waiting for a tragedy to ignite your desire to pray. Devote an equal amount of time to God when things are going well. Praise Him for the blessings and good times, because harder times are right around the corner. We also have to stop with the excuses. You know, the "I just don't have time to pray" excuses. Just like eating, prayer is something that should be done throughout the day. You don't need a special place or time. You can close your eyes and take a moment to silently connect with the Lord, no matter where you are. You better believe He receives those one-minute prayers, just as sure as He receives the long ones!

2. **Praying selfishly.** We often pray, hoping that God will accept our will, instead of showing us His. James 4:3 says, *"And when you do ask, you do not receive, because you ask with wrong motives, that you may squander it on your pleasures."* God will not give us something that we are not equipped to handle, regardless of how often we pray for that thing. We need to approach Him as humble children, seeking His

direction—not hoping that He will reroute us toward the destinations that we have chosen for ourselves. Praying for God's will to be done is truly allowing God to have *His* way in our lives on *His* terms. Although He cares about the desires of our heart, He is more interested in pushing us toward the purpose He has called us to. It is difficult for us to accept a "no" or "not now" from God, because we cannot see the whole picture of our lives. Remember that He knows what is in store for you, and walking in His will is the only way to obtain it.

3. **Praying in doubt.** When we approach God in prayer, we should have full faith and confidence that He will answer our prayers, according to His will. Matthew 7:7 says, *"Ask and it will be given to you; seek and you will find; knock and the door will be opened to you."* When we ask for something, we expect an answer in return. When we seek something, we expect to find it somewhere. When we knock on a door, we expect someone to open the door. We should, likewise, have the expectation that God will respond to our prayers. There is no prayer too big or small to bring before the Lord. He is the Creator of all things. What makes us think He is not able to answer our prayers? Hebrews 11:6 tells us, *"And without faith it is impossible to please God, because anyone who comes to him must believe that he exists and that he rewards those who earnestly seek him."* God frowns upon us when we do not have full faith and blessed assurance in His promises and abilities.

Challenge: From the three areas listed above, consider which category you struggle in the most. Make a personal plan to improve your area(s) of weakness.

What Satan whispers about prayer:
    "You need to have a certain amount of doubt so that you won't be disappointed."
    "Just pray for whatever you desire. You know what's best for you."
    "God has bigger things to be concerned about than your little problem. So don't waste your breath praying."

What God whispers about prayer:

> *"But let him ask in faith, with no doubting, for the one who doubts is like a wave of the sea that is driven and tossed by the wind" (James 1:6).*

> *"Likewise the Spirit helps us in our weakness. For we do not know what to pray for as we ought, but the Spirit himself intercedes for us with groanings too deep for words" (Romans 8:26).*

> *"Do not be anxious about anything, but in every situation, by prayer and petition, with thanksgiving, present your requests to God. And the peace of God, which transcends all understanding, will guard your hearts and your minds in Christ Jesus" (Philippians 4:6–7).*

Food for thought: How different would your days be if you scheduled a time each day to sit before the Lord in prayer, regardless of whether things are going well or not?

Prayer for us: Our Father in Heaven, we welcome You into our hearts as we pray right now. We thank You for having the wisdom that we need to navigate our lives. We do not know what we should pray for, but You intercede. Help our desires to align with Your will. And please help us to never make prayer a last priority in our lives. We treasure the opportunity to have a personal relationship and intimate conversations with You. In Your name we pray—Amen!

REJECTION

"Every rejection is incremental payment on your dues that in some way will be translated back into your work." —James Lee Burke

N othing stings quite like the pangs of rejection. Human beings have an innate desire to be accepted. Rejection is a culprit that can rob you of your confidence, leaving you to sulk in feelings of inadequacy and self-defeat. Sometimes the sting is surface level—rejection from a job or an opportunity. Other times, the sting seems to penetrate our souls—rejection from our close friends, our kids, our spouses, or other people in our family.

If dealing with rejection is one of your personal weaknesses, you better believe that Satan knows that it is an open door into your heart. He will attack you with rejection from people you never imagined would turn their backs to you. He wants you to feel alone. He wants you to label yourself as a failure—unaccepted, undesirable, unqualified, and unloved.

It can be difficult to know how to handle these feelings with positivity. Thankfully, Jesus Christ gave us the perfect example of handling rejection with grace. Isaiah 53:3 says, *"He was despised and rejected by men, a man of sorrows, and familiar with suffering."* In the midst of His rejection, Jesus persevered to continue His mission. We need to press on, with the attitude that something better awaits us. Our Lord is the only perfect man to have walked this earth—and yet, even He was rejected by multitudes of people. This should remind us that rejection is inevitable. No amount of "being enough" in this world will shield us from being rejected from something or someone. That is the bad news.

The good news is that rejection from this world does not have to cripple us, because we were *chosen.*

> *"But you are A CHOSEN RACE, A royal PRIEST-HOOD, A HOLY NATION, A PEOPLE FOR God's OWN POSSESSION, so that you may proclaim the excellencies of Him who has called you out of darkness into His marvelous light" (1 Peter 2:9).*

In order to deal with the pain of rejection, we have to keep perspective. We must recognize our worth in Christ. When we are unaccepted and turned away, we must find comfort in knowing that we have been adopted and welcomed by the King! It doesn't matter who said you were not wanted. It doesn't matter who deprived you of an opportunity. It doesn't matter who has left your side. No earthly rejection has the capacity to separate us from God's love. Furthermore, our Lord wants us to be around people and in places where we can be used for His glory. A rejection is often a stepping stone toward a person or place He sees better fit for us.

Dear sister, stop looking inward when you are rejected. Show yourself some grace. Remember that acceptance from human beings is not what draws you nearer to the cross and it sure won't get you to Heaven. Embrace God's love and acceptance for you. You are special, you have been set apart, and you were chosen by the One who matters most.

Challenge:
- Identify some instances in your life where you were rejected.
- What were you feeling at the time?
- What blessings or new opportunities resulted from your rejection?

What Satan whispers about rejection:
"Something must be wrong with you if you keep getting rejected. Nobody is in favor of you."

"Nobody can relate to the rejection you are feeling—the Lord was never rejected like this."

"This constant rejection will paralyze you. I don't know if you are strong enough to handle it."

What God whispers about rejection:

> *"What then, shall we say, in response to these things? If God is for us, who can be against us?" (Romans 8:31).*

> *"He was in the world, and the world was made through Him, and the world did not know Him. He came to His own, and His own did not receive Him" (John 1:10–11).*

> *"The steps of a good man are ordered by the LORD, and He delights in his way. Though he fall, he shall not be utterly cast down; for the LORD upholds him with His hand" (Psalm 37:23–24).*

Food for thought: How much of your rejection have you been blaming on yourself? What are some ways you can shift your focus away from your personal shortcomings?

Prayer for us: Dear God, You are faithful. You have chosen us and set us apart. You have had a plan for our lives, before we even existed. We thank You for acceptance through the blood of Jesus Christ. Please help us to remember that the world's opinions do not matter. We long to deal with rejection gracefully, just like Jesus did. Help us to move forward with good attitudes to the people and places where we can be used by You! In Your name we pray—Amen.

REPENTANCE

"How foolish to remain in prison when the door stands open." —Unknown

I magine that you are in a prison cell—confined to a small space, impregnable walls, limited freedom. You become a slave to mundane routines and days of constant supervision. You reflect on the series of crimes that carried you into this cold, isolating reality— wishing you would have done a few things differently. Suddenly, an officer approaches you to tell you that you are being released. You look at the officer in confusion. He explains that someone you never met has volunteered to take your place and serve time for you. You are certain that there must be a price you have to pay. But the officer assures you that the only thing you must do is to acknowledge the crimes you are responsible for and commit to not repeating those mistakes. The person taking your place is not expecting any repayment. You agree, take the necessary steps, and walk out of the prison—a guilty woman, who was given another chance and a clean slate, thanks to the grace of a stranger. Choosing a life of regret and imprisonment would have been a silly choice in comparison to a life of freedom.

Sin imprisons us in a similar way. We are confined to our guilty consciences, feelings of regret, and bruised hearts. We become slaves to the filth and shame of our actions, as we bury them away in our memories. We reflect on the things that we could have done differently to avoid our circumstances getting so bad—the lies that could have been truths, the wrath that could have been grace, the yeses that could have been nos. If only we would have made better choices, we would not feel so disgusted with ourselves.

God's word tells us that we have an open door to escape the turmoil of our sin. Jesus voluntarily paid the price for our sins by dying on the cross.

> *"He himself bore our sins in his body on the tree, that*
> *we might die to sin and live to righteousness. By his*
> *wounds you have been healed" (1 Peter 2:24).*

A perfect man, who we have never met, came to die in order to give those who are in Christ a clean slate when we repent of our sins. He asked for nothing in return for this blessing and the abundant life that it provides us. We simply have to acknowledge that we have sinned, repent before the Father, and commit to not being a repeated offender of our mistakes. And when we do fall short, the Lord is patient with us, shows us grace, and gives us more chances that we do not deserve.

> *"For by grace you have been saved through faith.*
> *And this is not your own doing; it is the gift of God"*
> *(Ephesians 2:8).*

How foolish we would be to not participate in this beautiful blessing of grace and repentance! When we avoid repentance, we deprive ourselves of abundant life. Even worse, we diverge from the path of truth that leads us to spending an eternity with Christ.

There are three common mistakes we make when it comes to repentance:

1. **Treating repentance as optional.** Repentance is not an option. It is consistently commanded throughout the Bible. This is a necessary part of spiritual growth and our salvation. Isaiah 59:2 says, *"But your iniquities have separated you from your God; your sins have hidden his face from you, so that he will not hear."* In the human relationships we cherish, we try to avoid letting things come between us and the people we love. Our relationship with God should be

treated the same way. Sin comes between us and the Father. Repentance is the only way to be reconciled to Him.

2. **Overlooking our own sin.** Oftentimes, we think that if we have not committed a "big sin," there is no need to repent. Romans 3:23 reminds us, *"For all have sinned and come short of the glory of God."* Sin begins in the heart. All of us have unclean hearts; therefore, we should all be repenting. Ask the Lord to survey your heart and forgive you for the unclean things that you may not be aware of. If we were perfect, sinless beings, we would not need a Savior.

3. **Failing to believe in the power of repentance.** Many of us repent with our mouths but then continue to carry the feelings of regret and shame. God designed repentance to free us of this self-defeat. If we truly believed in His power, we would accept the clean slate that He offers us through repentance. There is *no* sin too big for repentance to cover.

4. **Taking advantage of God's grace.** We often repent of a sin and find ourselves caught up in the same sin at some point. As human beings, we are imperfect. God recognizes our shortcomings and He is patient with us. However, we need to make sure we are making the best attempt we can to avoid repeating the sins that we repent of. This requires a thorough thought process of how we will avoid the particular sin, before we are tempted by it again. It can be especially difficult if the sin we are committing does not have immediate consequences that would lead us to want to stop. We should not need the threat of an immediate consequence to convince us to make a change. Continuing to live in sin in the absence of true repentance can result in irreversible consequences.

Challenge:
- Keep a daily repentance log where you can record the sins you are struggling with and repenting of.
- Review the log weekly. Are there sins that you are continuously having to repent of?

• What barriers are there that are preventing you from conquering the sin(s)? Make a game plan for how you plan to conquer the sin you seem to be struggling with consistently.

What Satan whispers about repentance:
"You don't have to repent. God knows your heart and that is enough."
"You're a good Christian, so God doesn't really care if you don't repent for little sins."
"Your sin is too big. Repentance is not enough for something that filthy."

What God whispers about repentance:

"No, I tell you; but unless you repent, you will all likewise perish" (Luke 13:5).

"Just so, I tell you, there will be more joy in heaven over one sinner who repents than over ninety-nine righteous persons who need no repentance" (Luke 15:7).

"The Lord is not slow to fulfill his promise as some count slowness, but is patient toward you, not wishing that any should perish, but that all should reach repentance" (2 Peter 3:9).

Food for thought: In what ways are your sins hindering you from a more abundant relationship with Christ?
Prayer for us: Our gracious Heavenly Father, You are so patient with us. Thank You for providing us with the opportunity to repent and be reconciled to You, no matter how many times we fall short. Lord, we do not want our sin to separate us from You. Please help us to repent of the ugliness of our hearts and our actions. Help us to never become too prideful for repentance. We recognize that we are imperfect and need You desperately. In Your name we pray—Amen.

SELF-CONTROL

"To handle yourself, use your head; to handle others, use your heart." —Eleanor Roosevelt

S elf-control can be a superpower when we exercise it regularly. If we could always control our impulses and actions, we would be invincible. Self-control is a key component of emotional intelligence, and it is also a fruit of the Holy Spirit.

> *"But the fruit of the Spirit is love, joy, peace, forbearance, kindness, goodness, faithfulness, gentleness and self-control. Against such things there is no law"* *(Galatians 5:22–23).*

Take a moment to conceptualize how amazing it is that the Holy Spirit dwells within us—guiding us and giving us the *choice* to influence our actions and outcomes. It is our natural instinct to make decisions based on our feelings and fleshly desires. Feelings and flesh tag team us and lead us to lash out on the people around us, eat those cookies and donuts that have been calling our names, make that purchase that we know we don't need, spend hours indulging in TV and social media, and entertain people and things that we know are no good for us.

We all recognize the benefits of self-control, but we often struggle to put our knowledge into action. When we are in the midst of a situation and it is time to act, self-control suddenly becomes more aspirational than accessible. Our willpower gets pushed to the back burner, and we focus on cooking up a main course of fleshly desires.

Challenge: There are several steps we can take to develop self-control and rely on it as a primary source of power rather than a last resort. Let us consider doing the following:

1. **Study and pray.** Proverbs 29:18 tells us, *"Where there is no revelation, the people cast off restraint."* We cannot put something into action without thoroughly understanding it. If you were told to change a tire for the first time, you would not know how to do it from instinct alone. After getting directions and practicing, you would become more efficient over time. The same applies to the acquisition of spiritual traits like self-control. As we soak up God's truths by reading His word, we can internalize the words and apply them to our daily situations. Sure, we won't get it right every time. But with persistence we will grow, until it becomes almost natural to us. Pray for the Holy Spirit to help you carry out these truths as you seek to study and improve.

2. **Choose a few alternative actions.** The human mind is pretty amazing. We have the ability to distract ourselves and redirect our thoughts anytime that we please. Unfortunately, we often abuse this power by using it to distract ourselves with insignificant things and avoid tasks we do not feel like doing. We can just as easily use this ability for good. We can make the choice to do an alternative action instead of the one we instinctively desire. For example, if you are triggered to respond to an insult from someone, you can choose a positive alternative like walking away or speaking words of life in return. Or if you are craving something that you know is bad for you, you can distract yourself by doing a chore or something else that is productive. As you contemplate your actions, ask yourself if the action is helpful or hurtful. It is either pushing you closer to God or pulling you farther away. *"So I say, walk by the Spirit and you will not gratify the desires of the flesh"* (Galatians 5:16). What are some practical ways you can distract yourself and redirect your attention to improve your self-control?

3. **Wait it out.** We often underestimate the power in waiting. We become slaves to our impulses by acting immediately in response to them. Our desires can wane over time. If there is something that your flesh is really pushing you to do, try waiting about twenty minutes. Notice how the burning desire changes as you have that time to reflect on the action and consequences.

4. **Celebrate small successes.** We tend to beat ourselves up when we fail to use self-control and deal with the consequences. We focus on our failures instead of our successes.

"How could I make that mistake again?"
"What was I thinking?"
"I knew better but chose to do it anyway."

Feeling defeated and being hard on ourselves does not move us any closer to the goal of practicing more self-control. We need to empower ourselves by identifying the exceptions. Think about a time where you were tempted to do or say something and you were able to successfully control yourself. What are some things that helped you to use self-control in that situation? Remind yourself that you can experience that success again.

What Satan whispers about self-control:
"It is too hard to use self-control in this situation."
"Having the desire to use more self-control is enough. God is content with that."
"I see other people fail to use self-control and it works out fine."
"It can't hurt to temporarily distract myself with something counter-productive."

What God whispers about self-control:

"No temptation has overtaken you except what is common to humankind. And God is faithful; he will not let you be tempted beyond what you can bear. But when you are tempted, he will also provide a way out so that you can endure it" (1 Corinthians 10:13).

141

"No, I strike a blow to my body and make it my slave so that after I have preached to others, I myself will not be disqualified for the prize" (1 Corinthians 9:27).

"Therefore, I urge you, brothers and sisters, in view of God's mercy, to offer your bodies as a living sacrifice, holy and pleasing to God—this is your true and proper worship. Do not conform to the pattern of this world, but be transformed by the renewing of your mind. Then you will be able to test and approve what God's will is—his good, pleasing and perfect will" (Romans 12:1–2).

"Be alert and of sober mind. Your enemy the devil prowls around like a roaring lion looking for someone to devour" (1 Peter 5:8).

Food for thought: Who would notice the change if you began using self-control regularly? What would they notice about you?

Prayer for us: Dear Lord, You are wonderful in all of Your ways. You have given us the fruit of the spirit of self-control to guide our lives and our actions. Lord, help us to develop self-control by studying and praying. Help us to be mindful of our actions and their consequences. Remove the desires within us that are contrary to Your word. We ask these things in Your name—Amen.

TRUSTING GOD

"Never be afraid to trust an unknown future to a known God." —Corrie Ten Boom

Have you ever played tug-of-war? The game can grow pretty intense as each team attempts to pull the rope in their direction. It can take a tremendous amount of persistence to win the game—especially if the opposing side is strong. After a while, something has got to give. The going gets tough for one team or the other, and the exhaustion begins to take toll. It is then that you have a winner and a loser.

Even if you have never played physical tug-of-war, I am willing to bet that you have played spiritual tug-of-war at some point in your life—you on one side of the rope, God on the other. God pulls you in one direction with bold signs and commandments. You pull away with all of your might, reluctant and disobedient. Sooner or later, you are exhausted, weary, and your hands are calloused. All that fighting back has gotten you nowhere, and God has the victory.

God does not want us to take the painful and dirty route to trusting Him. It is our own resistance that leads us to drag ourselves in the mud and be defeated. Instead, He wants us to forfeit. He is waiting for us to voluntarily surrender—acknowledging that He is stronger and more powerful than we could ever be.

"The Lord will fight for you; you need only to be still"
(Exodus 14:14).

We get ourselves in a frenzy when we lack control. This leads us to make two major mistakes. One mistake is taking matters into our own hands in an attempt to speed the process. The other mistake is trusting in other people for the answers and directions we should be seeking from God. God warns us against both of these mistakes.

1. **Trusting ourselves over God.** *"Those who trust in themselves are fools, but those who walk in wisdom are kept safe"* (Proverbs 28:26).

2. **Trusting others over God.** *"It is better to take refuge in the LORD than to trust in humans"* (Psalm 118:8)

We make all of these decisions, but we fail to consult our Father in Heaven. We don't get the results we want. Then we are discouraged, wondering why we have gotten nowhere. Seeking to control our situations will not get us an answer any faster and will not force God to change our circumstances. His will for our life is best and He is not interested in bargaining with us.

> *"'Ah, stubborn children,' declares the Lord, 'who carry out a plan, but not mine, and who make an alliance, but not of my Spirit, that they may add sin to sin'" (Isaiah 30:1).*

God has never been pleased with the stubborn attitudes and disobedience of humankind. Even as far back as in the Old Testament stories, we read of many negative consequences for people's lack of obedience and absolute trust. Remember that no matter how hard we pull in the opposite direction, God is stronger. If we do not truly trust in Him, how can we claim to be believers? My friend, please choose to surrender today to avoid causing yourself more pain tomorrow. Aren't you tired of trying to figure out your life?

Challenge:

- Write a short reflection about why you are not trusting God with your current situation. (Be transparent—He knows your heart).
- In reviewing the things you wrote, are your reasons logical?
- As a believer, what do these things reveal about your faith?

What Satan whispers about trusting:

"It is okay to try to change God's plans. You know what you need."
"What if you trust God and things don't turn out the way you want?"
"God is making a joke out of your life."

What God whispers about trusting:

"In their hearts, humans plan their course, but the LORD establishes their steps" (Proverbs 16:9).

"And we know that for those who love God all things work together for good, for those who are called according to his purpose" (Romans 8:28).

"For I know the plans I have for you," declares the LORD, "plans to prosper you and not to harm you, plans to give you hope and a future" (Jeremiah 29:11).

Food for thought: How much of your current stress is the result of trying to take life's matters into your hands as opposed to trusting in the Lord?

Prayer for us: Dear God, our futures are unknown, but You are all-knowing. Thank You for having a beautiful plan for our lives. You patiently wait for us to surrender. Please help us to let go and let You take control. Let us find comfort in knowing that the plans You have for Your children are good. We declare that You are working things out for our good—even right this moment. In Your name we pray—amen.

UNDERSTANDING

"You were made by God and for God and until you understand that, life will never make sense." — Unknown

Wouldn't it be nice if this whole "living as a Christian thing" were easy? If it were clear-cut, with no rough edges. If it meant that we could always trade confusion for clarity? Our walks with Christ have lots of detours, unpaved roads, and unknown destinations. As we encounter struggles, we begin to try to understand the purpose of it all. The difficult questions dance around in our minds:

"Why does God allow bad things to happen to good people?"

"Why won't God do something about all of the evil in our nation and world?"

"Why can't life be a little easier for Christians?"

"How can we be sure that a life in Christ is even worth it?"

We grow frustrated with our inability to neatly fit the puzzle pieces of our lives together. And oftentimes, we end up shaking a fist at God for not giving us the explanations we are seeking. We so desperately want Him to reveal just a little piece of the future so that we can be content!

Dear Sister, we need to remember that we were made *by* God — the same God who created the universe, the heavens, and the earth. He made us and knows our frustrations better than we know them. If He can keep the whole world running, what makes you think that He does not have a plan for you and me? More importantly, we were created *for* God. Our purpose on this Earth is not to live a life of comfort and perfection. We were created to glorify Him.

The reality is that God does not owe us any answers. If we could figure everything out on our own, serving God would have no purpose. We need to become less concerned with finding answers and more concerned with finding Christ. Our focus needs to shift from understanding the circumstances we are in to understanding what God wants us to learn in the midst of them.

> *"Trust in the Lord with all your heart and lean not on your own understanding. In all your ways, acknowledge him and he will make your paths straight" (Proverbs 3:5–6).*

> *"Do not be anxious about anything, but in every situation, by prayer and petition, with thanksgiving, present your requests to God. And the peace of God, which surpasses all understanding, will guard your hearts and your minds in Christ Jesus" (Philippians 4:6–7).*

You see, God never promised in His word that He would provide us with all of the answers that we want. But He does make it clear that in Him we find the peace we need to be content with lacking all of the answers. This type of peace allows our souls to be at rest, knowing that we will be provided with understanding when God sees fit. It is a blessed assurance that He has already taken care of the things that we are still trying to figure out.

Challenge: Reflect on a time when God gave you the peace you needed in regards to a difficult situation. Did you receive *all* of the answers in the situation? How were you able to be content with the answers you did receive?

What Satan whispers about understanding:
"How do you know God is working things out that you are trying to figure out? How can you be sure?"

"Christianity is not worth it if God won't give you understanding about what's happening in your life."

"Nothing that is happening makes sense. It is too confusing to bear."

What God whispers about understanding:

> *"Do you not know? Have you not heard? The LORD is the everlasting God, the Creator of the ends of the earth. He will not grow tired or weary, and his understanding no one can fathom" (Isaiah 40:28).*

> *"So we fix our eyes not on what is seen, but on what is unseen, since what is seen is temporary, but what is unseen is eternal" (2 Corinthians 4:18).*

> *"Jesus replied, 'You don't understand now what I am doing, but someday you will'"(John 13:7).*

Food for thought: Are you praying consistently for God's wisdom and discernment as it applies to your situation? Or are you spending more time in confusion than prayer?

Prayer for us: God, You are all-knowing and understand all things. Thank You for having a plan for the areas of our life that we are stressing over. Please teach us to lean on You in our confusion. We want to embrace the peace that You provide us. We desire to be content in knowing that You have things taken care of. Use us right where we are. In Your name we ask these things—Amen.

VENGEANCE

"He who seeks vengeance must dig two graves; one for his enemy and one for himself." —Chinese Proverb

Our society has become polluted with acts of evil, injustice, and ill will. It is easy to become discouraged from watching the news or following the tragedies via social media. There seems to be a diminishing to nonexistent regard for fellow humans. People respond to hatred with more hatred—throwing us into a perpetual cycle of evil and chaos and stifling the hope of positive progress.

While the malice that is crippling our society hurts us as a people, an even greater hurt stings us when we are victims of personal betrayal. When we are directly affected by wrongdoing, it can change us from the inside out. Knowing that somebody intentionally harmed us causes our flesh to automatically consider vengeance.

As Christians, we have been trained time and time again to show grace. But hurt that stings as deeply as personal betrayal and injustice erases the word "grace" from our mind's automatic responses. When the thought of vengeance comes to our minds, we sometimes begin to question our own morals and think we are "such bad Christians" for even thinking about repaying someone for wrongdoing. Even as Christians, we are not wired in such a way that we do not desire to avenge. Although we may not naturally choose to avoid vengeance, we can make the choice out of obedience to God.

Challenge: There are a few things that we must remember when "turning the other cheek" seems difficult to impossible. Consider how the following steps can improve your situation.

1. **Remember who the REAL enemy is.**
   When we are in conflict and want to repay someone for the evil they have done, Satan is gloating. Few things please him more than leading us against one another so that we are distracted from him—the one who is really behind all of the confusion. Ephesians 6:12 reminds us, *"For our struggle is not against flesh and blood, but against the rulers, against the authorities, against the powers of this dark world and against the spiritual forces of evil in the heavenly realms."* What a powerful reminder—to know that other human beings are not where the true problem lies. Satan is crafty and ready to use any divisive schemes necessary to lead you to evil. Refuse to allow him to coerce you into the sin of vengeance.

2. **Remember where your trust should be.**
   There is no perfect person on this Earth. Because of our carnal nature, letting others down is inevitable. When you begin to put this into perspective, you realize that wanting to avenge someone for wronging you is pointless. Just as that person has wronged you, I am certain that you have wronged someone else at some point in life—intentionally or inadvertently. Psalm 146:3 says, "Do not put your trust in princes, in human beings, who cannot save. When they breathe their last, they return to the earth, and all their plans die with them." As long as we put our trust into humankind, we will be disappointed. Instead, we have to keep our eyes on the One who has overcome the world. This will give us the heart change we need to reconsider vengeance.

3. **Ask yourself what vengeance will accomplish.**
   Is what you are planning to do helpful or hurtful? This is not only applicable to major acts of vengeance, like physically harming or sabotaging someone. An equal danger is found in the subtle acts of vengeance that we choose to participate in—gossiping to hurt someone's reputation, talking to them with a nasty attitude, treating them in the unkind manner in

which they treated us. Consider what will be accomplished by these actions. Will responding in such a manner benefit you? Or will it continue rob you of your joy and deplete your positive energy?

Walk in love.

Throughout the Bible, we are commanded to love. In fact, Christ labeled it as the greatest command. Nowhere in the Bible does it say that our love should be conditional. Genuine love towards others is not contingent upon the way that they treat us. That means that we are required to love even when vengeance seems more appropriate and natural. 1 Thessalonians 5:15 directs us to, *"Make sure that nobody pays back wrong for wrong, but always strive to do what is good for each other and for everyone else."* It might upset you to notice that there is no comma or semi-colon followed by, *"if* the person didn't hurt you that bad" or *"if* the person apologized." As Christians, we must walk in love consistently, in spite of our circumstances.

What Satan says about vengeance:

"They did you wrong first, so vengeance is okay. They asked for it."

"How will they ever get what they deserve if you don't show them?"

"Vengeance is a normal and acceptable part of anger. People do it all the time."

What God says about vengeance:

"You have heard that it was said, 'Eye for eye, and tooth for tooth.' But I tell you, do not resist an evil person. If anyone slaps you on the right cheek, turn to them the other cheek also" (Matthew 5:38–39).

"It is mine to avenge; I will repay. In due time their foot will slip; their day of disaster is near and their doom rushes upon them" (Deuteronomy 32:35).

"In your anger do not sin: Do not let the sun go down
while you are still angry, and do not give the devil
a foothold" (Ephesians 4:26–27).

Food for thought: Consider a time you took it upon yourself to avenge someone. What did you gain from it? What would you gain from avenging this time?

Prayer for us: Our Lord and Savior, You are mighty. Thank You for reminding us that You will respond to evil-doing in Your time and in Your way. Help us to remember that vengeance is not our responsibility. We know that sin separates us from You. We do not want to fall victim to our emotions and make hurtful decisions. We want to walk patiently in love, even when it is difficult. We need Your help, desperately. In Your name we pray—Amen.

WEARINESS

"When you face the perils of weariness, carelessness, and confusion, don't pray for an easier life. Pray instead to be a stronger man or woman of God." — Luis Palau

W hat a place of discomfort and discontentment — soul depleted of energy, mind restless. Stuck in between the days of past and future — good times seeming out of reach in either direction. Searching for positivity takes every ounce of energy you have left. So sometimes you choose to do nothing, out of lack of knowing what to do.

There are many currents that carry us into bleak and weary days. Which ones are keeping you spinning in the vicious cycle?

Challenge: Consider which area(s) of your life might be making you weary. After you have identified the relevant area(s), use the given suggestions to create a plan to overcome weariness.

Are you weary because you are avoiding change?

Sometimes we get stuck in routines or habits that yield no profitable results. We do the same things over and over again, and we don't get any further ahead. Maybe it is happening at work — mundane days on the job, feeling stuck. Maybe it is happening at school — lack of success and increased uncertainty about the purpose in being there. Maybe it is happening in personal relationships — no progress in friendship, marriage, parenthood. *Consider this:* Sometimes, the solution to weariness cannot be found until we step out of our comfort zones and make a change. We have to be honest with ourselves if what we have been trying is not working. Then, we must take a deep look inward—no pointing fingers at others for our weariness. We have the choice to make changes that will give us the peace we desire. But we can't make these changes without consulting God first. Pray consistently for God to show you which opportunities, people, and things are meant for you. Ask Him to help you focus on and change the things that are in your control. Only God can provide the insight we need in our decision-making processes. *"He cuts off every branch in me that bears no fruit, while every branch that does bear fruit he prunes so that it will be even more fruitful" (John 15:2).*

Are you weary because you are suffering from spiritual malnutrition?

Have you ever seen a plant that doesn't get the nourishment it needs to thrive and grow? If it exists in the absence of water and sunlight, it does not last very long. You watch it wither—dry up, droop, leaves sail away. The same thing happens to our souls when we are not spiritually fed. *Consider this:* We feed our spiritual life by reading God's word, praying to Him, and being encouraged by other brothers and sisters in Christ. If our souls have been starved of these things, it becomes more evident with each attack from Satan. Every time we get burdened with something new, we are chopped down another inch. Eventually, we are unable to stand without growing faint. Having a healthy spiritual life will not prevent us from getting attacked. However, it will give us the strength we need to overcome the attacks gracefully. We will be like the strong plants described in the book of Jeremiah. *"They are like trees planted along a riverbank, with roots that reach deep into the water. Such trees are not bothered by the heat or worried by long months of drought. Their leaves stay green, and they never stop producing fruit" (Jeremiah 17:2).* In what areas should you consider nourishing yourself spiritually?

Are you weary because you've neglected your personal needs?

For many folks, weariness manifests unconsciously. The weariness starts off as an innocent trait called, "caring." Time is dedicated to caring for friends, caring for spouses, caring for children, caring for sick loved ones, caring for everyone—except yourself. Before you know it, you have been stretched, pulled, and overextended. Selflessness is a beautiful attribute when it is demonstrated with balance. *Consider this:* Before we dedicate ourselves to sacrificing for everyone else, we must remember that we are to be a sacrifice to Christ. Romans 12:1 says, *"Therefore, I urge you, brothers and sisters, in view of God's mercy, to offer your bodies as a living sacrifice, holy and pleasing to God—this is your true and proper worship."* Being a living sacrifice to God requires making sure that our personal needs are met. If we are not healthy, we cannot be effective in helping others. What areas of your health (physical, spiritual, emotional, mental) have you neglected in the midst of serving others? Make a personal goal for achieving balance.

Are you weary because of an earthly circumstance that is out of your control?

Earthly troubles like illness and loss can make us grow extremely weary—especially when these cards are dealt to us unexpectedly. In such cases, we may feel cheated and overlooked, as if God has forgotten about us. *Consider this:* Remembering that Christ is fighting the battle with us can help us to not be consumed in weariness. He has overcome the troubles of this world (John 16:33). He came so that we could have an abundant life in the midst of our circumstances (John 10:10). And He will never leave our side (Hebrews 13:5). Romans 8:38–39 says, *"For I am sure that neither death nor life, nor angels nor rulers, nor things present nor things to come, nor powers, nor height nor depth, nor anything else in all creation, will be able to separate us from the love of God in Christ Jesus our Lord."*

What Satan whispers about weariness:
"There is no point in continuing because things are not getting any better."

"You don't really have to pray or study. How do you even know that's making a difference? Do it on your own."

"It will be this way forever—weary and bleak."

What God whispers about weariness:

"And let us not grow weary of doing good, for in due season we will reap, if we do not give up" (Galatians 6:9).

"Have you not known? Have you not heard? The LORD is the everlasting God,

the Creator of the ends of the earth. He does not faint or grow weary; his understanding is unsearchable. He gives power to the faint, and to him who has no might he increases strength. Even youths shall faint and be weary, and young men shall fall exhausted; but they who wait for the LORD shall renew their strength; they shall mount up with wings like eagles; they shall run and not be weary; they shall walk and not faint" (Isaiah 40:28–31).

"For I consider that the sufferings of this present time are not worth comparing with the glory that is to be revealed to us" (Romans 8:18).

Food for thought: A major part of recovering from a weary soul is believing that better days lie ahead. How can your understanding of the temporary nature of this earthly life help you find hope in the better days to come?

Prayer for us: Dear God, You are strong when we are weak and weary. We thank You that You have already conquered every worldly trial and tribulation. We know that we cannot do life without You! Please lift up our weary souls and give us the strength and hope we need to move forward. Satan wants to use bleak circumstances to deter us, but we declare that he will not steal our joy! Please continue to order our steps and mold us into stronger servants for You. In Your name we ask these things—Amen.

CPSIA information can be obtained
at www.ICGtesting.com
Printed in the USA
LVOW01s2157171216
517778LV00031B/561/P